everything arises, everything falls away

everything arises, everything falls away

TEACHINGS ON
IMPERMANENCE
AND THE END OF
SUFFERING

AJAHN CHAH

Translated by PAUL BREITER

SHAMBHALA
Boston & London
2005

Shambhala Publications, Inc.
Horticultural Hall
300 Massachusetts Avenue
Boston, Massachusetts 02115
www.shambhala.com

9 8 7 6 5 4 3 2 1

FIRST EDITION
Printed in the United States of America

♾ This edition is printed on acid-free paper that meets
the American National Standards Institute z39.48 Standard.

Distributed in the United States by Random House, Inc.,
and in Canada by Random House of Canada Ltd

Library of Congress Cataloging-in-Publication Data
Chah, Achaan.
Everything arises, everything falls away: teachings on
impermanence and the end of suffering / Ajahn Chah; translated by
Paul Breiter.—1st ed.
p.   cm.
ISBN 1-59030-217-6 (alk. paper)
1. Impermanence (Buddhism) 2. Suffering—Religious aspects—Buddhism.
3. Buddhism—Doctrines. I. Breiter, Paul. II. Title.
BQ4261.C43 2005
294.3'422—dc22
2004016050

Dedicated to Ajahn Chah's Sangha of
ordained disciples, men and women
who live the teachings every day

CONTENTS

TRANSLATOR'S PREFACE

IN 1954, AJAHN CHAH (1918–1992) and a handful of disciples established a monastery in a remote forest in northeast Thailand. Leading the simple life of ascetic forest monks much the same as the Buddha did some 2,500 years earlier, his compassionate presence and direct and lucid teaching style attracted countless thousands of lay and monastic followers, and monasteries grew up like mushrooms throughout Thailand and the West. Showing us the immediacy of the Dharma, Ajahn Chah demystified the concepts of Buddhism so that almost anyone who listened could get the point. He taught villagers how to manage their family lives and finances, yet he might be just as likely to tell them about practicing to realize nirvana. He could instruct a visiting group he was meeting for the first time on the basics of morality, without moralizing and in a way that was uplifting, while gently reminding them of their mortality and infusing them with his infectious happiness. Or, he might scold the daylights out of local monastics and laypeople. He could start a discourse by expounding the most basic Buddhist ideas and seemingly without changing tone move on to talking about emptiness.

Ajahn Chah wasn't a stickler for consistency in use of terminology. He didn't speak from notes and never planned the contents of a talk. But he made the teachings practical and accessible. To the unlearned, he would say, "Never mind thinking about the aggregates, about form, feeling, perception, thought, and consciousness. So many things! Just say, 'body and mind.' That's enough." Though he didn't often quote the scriptures, he could explain abstruse terms when he needed to. The "Discourse on the Foundations of Mindfulness," for example, talks of "seeing the body in the body," and likewise for the other aggregates. Ajahn Chah simply said, "When we recognize the body as impermanent, unsatisfactory, and not us or ours, that is called 'seeing the body in the body.'"

Sometimes he emphasized the three characteristics of insight meditation—impermanence, unsatisfactoriness, and lack of self—sometimes the Four Noble Truths, but these were tools pointing at something beyond. When the Buddha first began teaching, he said, "Opened are the doors to the deathless. Those with ears to hear, release your faith." Ajahn Chah explained this somewhat mysterious concept of "not dying" in practical fashion in the light of *anatta,* not-self: when there is no "I" and no "mine," then there is no one to die. The aggregates of existence appear and pass away, but not placing ourselves in them or believing that they are us or ours, we don't die with them and thus have no suffering over them. He also explained it as no longer being born and dying with the external and internal happenings we experience—that is to say, liberation.

But more than anything else, Ajahn Chah grounded his teaching in *anicca,* impermanence, as the initial focus of mindfulness practice. It is the key that opens the door and gives entrance to the Dharma, and it leads the mind to see the other facets of experience.

In keeping with the spirit of change and uncertainty, surprises were always in store in the way he taught and the way he trained his students. He frequently altered the routine in his monastery. He wasn't easy to pin down or classify. He often emphasized monastic life as the best way to practice, pointing out its many advantages, yet he gave profound teachings to laypeople and showed real respect for anyone with a sincere interest, anyone who made effort in practice, saying on many occasions that ordaining or not ordaining is beside the point. His treatment of the monastic discipline could be puzzling. But putting his instructions into practice can bring us to direct experience and a place of certainty.

Sometimes he spoke of the need for *samadhi,* meditative stability, and explained the progression through the states of absorption (*jhana*). At other times he downplayed tranquillity and warned of its dangers as a sidetrack. In his meditation teaching, mindfulness was central. Whether the mind is tranquil or agitated, focused or scattered, the meditator can be aware of its conditions and recognize the nature of their appearance and disappearance, and through that come to recognize something beyond mental activity.

Anicca, Dukkha, and Anatta

When the Buddha taught his second sermon, the "Discourse on the Characteristic of Not-Self," he brought his five disciples to full enlightenment by explaining the progression of insight through the three characteristics of existence, *anicca, dukkha,* and *anatta.* This teaching was grounded in pointing out the obvious, that everything in body and mind is impermanent. What is impermanent is by its nature not satisfactory, and the unstable and unsatisfactory doesn't merit being considered ourselves or our own. Through questions and answers, the Buddha led his disciples to this understanding, and he further explained that seeing things in this light brings about dispassion and detachment, freeing the mind.

This approach to understanding, beginning with the unreliability of all we experience, was a main emphasis of Ajahn Chah's teaching and training. With the immovability of a master of Dharma combat, he cut through disciples' complexities and attachments, whether in relation to the outer world, their own bodies, or states of meditation, by reminding them, "It's not permanent. It's not certain." Though a child can say the words, when spoken from a place of conviction they become vivid indicators of the truth and the way to freedom.

Impermanence (*anicca*) is usually pointed out as the first of the three characteristics because it is the most obvious, and it is this fact that Ajahn Chah comes back to again and again as the foundation of correct view and the entrance to the path. He also spoke of it as uncertainty, pointing out this quality of existence when reminding people not to take things too seriously: ups and downs, gain and loss are unavoidable, and our own perceptions of what is good and what is bad can change, so such an understanding can bring equanimity in the trials of daily life as well as in meditation. When all is unstable and unreliable, how can it be considered real? Leaving ourselves at the mercy of changeable phenomena and relying on them for happiness is a sure formula for disaster.

Dukkha is usually translated as "suffering." Unhappy experiences such as loss and separation from the beloved, association with the unpleasant, sorrow, illness, and death are obvious forms of dukkha. It is also spoken of as the pervasive and inherent unsatisfactoriness of all we can experience; more specifically, it refers to experience based on the delusion of believing things to be real, permanent, and belonging to, constituting, or somehow relating to a self. According to Buddhist teaching, the real problem lies not in natural and unavoidable occurrences, in the loss that follows gain or the parting that follows meeting, but in the mental activity built upon them. Such adds more suffering, and that is avoidable. Through reflection and direct realization in meditation, one can see how holding on to any object or experience causes tension, frustration, and despair, since nothing can last forever.

Ajahn Chah also taught about dukkha in the framework of the Four Noble Truths: suffering, its origination, its cessation, and the path leading to cessation. "When you want to enter a house, you go in through the door. When you want to enter the Dharma, you go in through recognizing the fact of dukkha," he would say. His teaching may occasionally seem heavy with mention of dukkha, but he teaches about four truths, not one. He reminds us that there is a goal and that there can be an end of suffering once and for all, and that living in freedom and happiness is indeed possible for all who apply themselves. It is the recognition of the unsatisfactory nature of existence, with all the sufferings that get compounded as we move through life, that impels us to seek the way to liberation. This recognition leads to disenchantment with the way we always lived and saw things and to dispassion and detachment toward the enticements of worldly life.

Ajahn Chah often spoke of *anatta,* not-self, in the simplest terms, starting with the bare facts of our physical bodies. They don't obey our commands, and in the end they desert us. Sometimes he emphasized how they are subject to aging, illness, and death, while sometimes he spoke of them as mere collections of the elements of earth, water, fire, and air, in which no person can be found. As the scripture says, that which is impermanent and unreliable and thus of an unsatisfactory nature is certainly not worthy of being called oneself or one's own.

In teaching meditation, Ajahn Chah repeatedly spoke of seeing the arising and ceasing of mental activity, but he added that this is not all there is to the matter. In *Being Dharma* he says,

At first we have to see impermanence, unsatisfactoriness, and lack of self as the nature of the mind. But the truth is that there is really nothing there. It is empty. We see arising and passing away, but actually nothing is arising and passing away. We see the arising and ceasing by relying on perception and conceptualization. . . . It is not merely arising and passing away. The result will be recognition of your true mind. You will still experience arising and ceasing, but you won't be drawn to happiness, and suffering cannot follow you then.

Ajahn Chah gives us the "bad news" about the shortcomings of ordinary worldly existence and shows renunciation as the key, yet his only aim is liberation. As he said, "Making offerings, listening to teachings, practicing meditation, whatever we do should be for the purpose of developing wisdom. Developing wisdom is for the purpose of liberation, freedom from all conditions and phenomena."

The Man and His Methods

Ajahn Chah never taught from texts or notes or planned his teachings. He was always spontaneous, though sometimes he found himself with nothing to say to certain people; he remarked that it probably meant there was no karmic connection between them, or that such people didn't have the karma to hear spiritual teaching. Speaking about how the teachings came to him, he quoted the Buddha. At one time the Buddha gave a discourse to his disciples and then asked if they had ever heard those words before. They replied that they had not, and the Buddha said that he too was just hearing them for the first time.

Ajahn Chah didn't recommend a lot of reading or study, especially for his Western disciples. "You've been studying all your lives, and where has it gotten you?" he would demand of us. And he often said, "If you have a bachelor's degree, you suffer on the level of a bachelor. If you have a master's degree, you become a master of suffering. If you have a doctorate, you suffer on the level of a doctor." While he could infuse the most basic instructions with his joyfulness, he sometimes told people things they didn't want to hear.

When he was at the Insight Meditation Society in Massachusetts in 1979, one night he gave a Dharma talk that focused mostly on *sila,* moral conduct. At the end, he apologized for scolding the meditators so badly, and said, "I didn't want to say these things, but the Buddha told me to!" The tension broke, and the meditation hall filled with laughter.

Disciples and visitors would present Ajahn Chah with every-thing from the sublime to the outlandish. Some wanted to discuss fine points of scripture, some wanted to argue, some laid their bur-dens and worries great and small at his feet. He was usually able to avoid argument and get sharply to the point in a way that was not confrontational but that handed the matter back to the questioner for deeper reflection.

A Thai man who'd been a monk for several years at Wat Pah Pong, Ajahn Chah's principal monastery in Thailand, later disrobed and became an alcoholic and ruffian, but would still come to see his former abbot. One day he announced that he wanted to join the army and start killing communists; since they were a threat to Thai society, it wouldn't really be wrong. Instead of lecturing him, Ajahn Chah simply said, "Well, if it's OK for you to kill commu-nists, I guess it's OK for someone to kill you."

Convinced that he must have the power to know winning lot-tery numbers, laypeople were always directly or indirectly asking Ajahn Chah to let them in on the jackpot. Rather than lecturing them on the foolishness of this, he would simply say things like, "If I could see the numbers, I'd tell my relatives so they could all get rich. Why should I tell you?"

Ajahn Chah gave this example of answering questions in a way that is most helpful to the questioner:

Once on his ascetic wanderings he was staying alone in a de-serted monastery. Some villagers came one day and asked if they could pick the fruit growing there. Ajahn Chah told them, "Folks, I'm not the abbot of this place. I've just come to stay here for a while. I can't forbid you to pick the fruit, and I can't permit you to pick it, either."

Hearing his words, the people were stumped. After discussing it among themselves, they finally said, "If it's like that, we won't take the fruit," and went on their way.

The Forest Tradition and Its Teachers

Ajahn Chah was frank about his own difficulties when he first became a meditation monk trying to adjust to the ascetic way of life. Instructing the community on the rules of training, he showed his empathy for those who had a hard time with the simple but arduous routine. Taking food only once a day, the monks and novices rise at 3:00 a.m. for meditation, go on a walk of an hour or two for alms at daybreak, then come back and sit in silence until the food is distributed and the meal can begin. The abbot commences eating, and then each one after him starts in turn, while the hungry fellows at the end of the line squirm, often with stomachs growling and saliva flowing. Ajahn Chah told his disciples that he too struggled with the monastic discipline.

> I'd think, "Hey, why don't the monks at the head of the line start eating already? What's taking those guys?" I'd curse the senior monks. "Let me be the elder just once! I would start eating right away so the others wouldn't have to wait like this!"
>
> I went through this. I would sit there waiting to eat and look at the *ajahn* (teacher). I'd be looking and looking, but he wouldn't eat. He was training us. He'd be joking with the laypeople, while I'd be thinking, "Hey! We're going to die here!" Sometimes I thought, "If I ever disrobe, it would be because of this! I can't stay here and put up with this. I need to eat when I'm hungry. It would be better to live at home . . . it would be better to live anywhere!"

Occasionally he spoke of the early days at Wat Pah Pong, in the 1950s, a time when rural Thailand and especially the northeast were poor and undeveloped and conditions in the monastery were extremely harsh: meager food, wading through deep water to get to the villages for alms, rampant malaria with no treatment available, lack of the most basic supplies. One year, a married couple whose nephew was living at the monastery with Ajahn Chah decided to ordain and join him at Wat Pah Pong. But they found the life too hard and soon disrobed and returned to the city. Ajahn Chah told the story:

> Experiencing the conditions in the monastery and the life of meditation monks really got them down. After they disrobed, when they talked about the way we lived here, the lady would start crying. People who hadn't lived like this had no idea about it. Eating once a day, was that making progress or falling behind? I don't know what to call it.
>
> Nobody came to visit. Even dogs couldn't bear to stay here. The *kutis* [monastic dwellings] were far apart and far from the meeting place. After everything was done at the end of the day, we separated and entered the forest to go to our kutis to practice. That made the dogs afraid they wouldn't have any safe place to stay. So they would follow the monks into the forest, but when they went up into their kutis, the dogs would be left alone and felt afraid, so they would try to follow other monks, but those monks would also disappear into their kutis.
>
> I thought about this sometimes: even the dogs can't bear it, but still we live here! Pretty extreme. It made me a little melancholy, too.
>
> But there was some point to this ascetic life. When we aren't yet skilled in practice, if the body is too comfortable the mind gets out of control. When a fire starts and the wind blows, it spreads the fire and the house burns down.

The lineage of Ajahn Chah, and Ajahn Mun before him, is called the Forest Tradition. Not too long ago, Thailand was 70 percent forested; at present, it's probably closer to 10 percent. Ajahn Chah watched the forests disappear during his lifetime. Among the many benefits and blessings he saw in the forest monastery tradition was the preservation of patches of forest. He often praised the simple life in the forest for its conduciveness to meditation and even waxed lyrical at times:

> The Buddha was born in the forest. Born in the forest, he studied Dharma in the forest. He taught in the forest, beginning with the Discourse on the Turning of the Wheel of Dharma. He entered nirvana in the forest.
>
> It's good for those of us who are interested in this tradition to understand the forest. Living in the forest doesn't mean that our minds become wild, like those of forest animals. Our minds can become elevated and spiritually noble. Living in the city, we live among distraction and disturbance. In the forest, there is quiet and tranquillity. We can contemplate things clearly and develop wisdom. So we take this quiet and tranquillity as our friend and helper. Such an environment is conducive to Dharma practice, so we take it as our dwelling place; we take the mountains and caves for our refuge.
>
> Observing natural phenomena, wisdom comes about in such places. We learn from and understand trees and everything else, and it brings about a state of joy. The sounds of nature we hear don't disturb us. We hear the birds calling, as they will, and it is actually a great enjoyment. We don't react with any aversion, and we aren't thinking harmful thoughts. We aren't speaking harshly or acting aggressively toward anyone or anything. Hearing the sounds of the forest gives delight to the mind; even as we are hearing sounds, the mind is tranquil.

The times Ajahn Chah spoke about his teachers and other masters of the lineage revealed common qualities of directness and simplicity. Eschewing Buddhist terminology, they provoked investigation on the part of the listener, using the objects and vocabulary of everyday life. Ajahn Mun (1870–1950) was certainly the most renowned master of his day and is largely credited with reviving the meditation tradition of forest-dwelling monastics. Ajahn Chah spent only a few days with him but afterward always spoke of himself as a disciple of Ajahn Mun, saying, "If a person with good eyes stands close to something, he sees it. If his eyes are bad, it doesn't matter how long he's there." Among the things Ajahn Mun clarified for him was the nature of mind, pointing out the difference between the mind itself and its changeable states and activities, and this book begins with this explanation as the foundation of right understanding.

One of Ajahn Chah's oft-repeated stories concerned a man who decided to "leave it all behind" and follow the Dharma. He sold his home and possessions and had his family ordain with him. They went on pilgrimage to India, and then returned to Thailand to practice under a spiritual master.

Ajahn Mun being Thailand's best-known teacher, they went to his monastery. Upon arriving, they found him sitting with his disciples, chewing betel nut, talking and laughing. The man was shocked and dismayed, as this didn't fit his idea of what a guru should look like: he thought about the scriptures, where it was said that the Buddha never laughed, but only smiled without showing his teeth. So he and his family left Ajahn Mun, disrobed, and gave up the quest.

Two other teachers Ajahn Chah spoke of with reverence were Ajahn Kinnaree and Ajahn Tongrat (whose teaching style is displayed in "A Fish Story"). And there were patron saints of the lineage, such as the reclusive Ajahn Sao, Ajahn Mun's mentor and senior companion, who during Ajahn Chah's childhood once came to stay in the nearby forest where Ajahn Chah later founded his monastery.

"My father went to hear the Dharma from him. I was a child, but the memory stuck in my mind always," Ajahn Chah recalled.

"My father told me how he went to pay respects to this meditation monk. It was the first time he saw a monk eating out of his bowl, putting everything together in the one almsbowl—rice, curry, sweet, fish, everything. It made him wonder what kind of monk this might be.

"Then he told me about getting Dharma teachings from Ajahn Sao. It wasn't the ordinary way of teaching; he just said what was on his mind. That was the practice monk who came to stay here once."

In Ajahn Chah's monasteries, the emphasis was on making all activities into meditation; likewise, he pointed out that teaching could be found everywhere, and that in particular, everything a meditation master did was imparting instruction. In his informal style of teaching, Ajahn Chah would occasionally work vignettes of these masters into his discourses:

> Please understand that everything in our way of life is for training and awakening the mind. Whatever the Ajahn does, all his actions and speech, whether it seems gentle or harsh, is for this purpose. It's all Dharma teaching. New people don't understand this. When we say that the Ajahn is giving teaching, they think it means he'll get up on the high seat and talk. That's what teaching Dharma means to them. And then when the Ajahn does that, as soon as he recites the homage to the Buddha at the beginning of the talk, they fall asleep!
>
> In the past I stayed with Ajahn Kinnaree. I often didn't understand what he was talking about. Whenever someone did something that wasn't right, he would shout, "Hey, you're going to hell!" When we were eating, he'd say, "You over there, you just dropped into hell!" I thought he was obsessed; I didn't know why he was always going on about hell. Whatever we did, he always told us we were dropping into hell. But as I kept on hearing it, I tried to contemplate the meaning. What

was this hell talk all about? "You just fell into hell!" "Watch out! You're going to drop into hell!" So finally I went and asked him.

"Oh, it means you're on your way there; you're creating the cause for dukkha. Don't make causes for dukkha! That's where hell is! That's where you'll fall."

Hearing these words, I finally got it: just dukkha itself is hell. Oh! But even something this obvious I wasn't able to figure out by myself. Suffering is hell. Someone who is doing wrong and creating suffering for himself is a hell-being. Thinking it over, I could understand that this is where hell is. It's so close and immediate like this.

Ajahn Tongrat, a senior disciple of Ajahn Sao and Ajahn Mun, was known as an unconventional master whose words and behavior often appeared strange to others. Ajahn Chah held him up as an example of someone who got to the heart of the matter, and the way of life in Ajahn Chah's monasteries was modeled in large part after that in Ajahn Tongrat's.

Ajahn Tongrat didn't teach a lot; he always told us, "Be careful! Be really careful!" That's how he taught. "If you're not really careful, you'll take it on the chin!" This is truly how it is. Even if he didn't say it, it's still how it is: if you're not careful, you'll take it on the chin.

Usually we aren't aware of the ways in which teachers are giving Dharma. Once Ajahn Tongrat was walking with a group of monks. He saw a male buffalo eating grass by the roadside. He said, "Oh! This female buffalo is eating grass near the road!" The monks were startled, and they wondered if Ajahn Tongrat had mistaken a male buffalo for a female.

They walked on for a while, and then he said, "Hey, did you see that female buffalo eating grass?" The monks probably thought the ajahn was confused. They didn't understand that he was teaching them something. Someone with wisdom, upon hearing these words, would have understood. Buffalo aren't "male" or "female." Calling them such is only a convention. But we designate them as male and female and then cling firmly to that as being something ultimately true.

But we tend to be like that. For example, when you see a woman, your mind changes in one way. If you see a man, your mind reacts in another way. If you see an old person, it will change in another way, and if you see a young person, it changes in yet another way. This is only the path of suffering. You are attracted to the young but repelled by the old, attracted by beautiful people and un-interested in plain or ugly people. Thus the mind is con-tinuously creating karma and dukkha.

So just walking along, the ajahn is teaching us. When he speaks about various things, he is teaching us. We should understand this and recognize the Dharma. Dharma is everywhere.

A technical note on terminology: Pali is the language of the Theravada scriptures, but Sanskrit versions of some terms that are likely to be familiar to Western readers have been used here; thus, "Dharma" instead of "Dhamma," "nirvana" instead of "nibbana," "karma" instead of "kamma." In other instances, it was more ap-propriate to use Pali. A glossary appears at the end of the book.

Teachings quoted in the preface were translated from tapes, re-called from formal talks and informal conversations in the 1970s at which I was present, or passed on by other disciples of Ajahn Chah. The teachings in the book are all taken from a collection of some 150 tapes in the Thai and Lao languages that somehow survived the ravages of time and the tropics. The talks were given to the monas-tic community and to laypeople, at Ajahn Chah's monasteries and other locations in Thailand, and in England and the United States.

Some chapters relate anecdotes about Ajahn Chah and his disciples. They are not spoken in his voice but are identified with his name in the title, such as "That's Good Too: Ajahn Chah's View."

An error in converting dates from the Buddhist dating system previously led to Ajahn Chah's date of birth being given as 1919. It should be 1918.

PART ONE

RIGHT VIEW

1

—

Understanding Mind

IN MEDITATION PRACTICE, WE work to develop mindfulness so that we will be constantly aware. Working with energy and patience, the mind can become firm. Then whatever sense phenomena we experience, whether agreeable or disagreeable, and whatever mental phenomena such as reactions of gladness or dejection, we will see them clearly. Phenomena are one thing, and the mind is another. They are separate matters.

When something contacts the mind and we are pleased by it, we want to pursue it. When something is displeasing, we want to escape from it. This is not seeing the mind, but running after phenomena. Phenomena are phenomena, mind is mind. We have to separate them and recognize what the mind is and what phenomena are. Then we can be at ease.

When someone speaks harshly to us and we get angry, it means that we are deluded by phenomena and are following after them; the mind is caught by its objects and follows after its moods. Please understand that all these things we experience externally and internally are nothing but deceptions. They are nothing certain or true, and pursuing them, we lose our way. The Buddha wanted us to meditate and see the truth of them, the truth of the world. The world is the phenomena of the six senses; phenomena are the world.

If we don't understand the Dharma, if we don't know the mind and don't know phenomena, then the mind and its objects get mixed together. Then we experience suffering and feel that our minds are suffering. We feel our minds are wandering, uncontrollably experiencing different unhappy conditions, changing into different states. That's not really the case: there aren't many minds, but many phenomena. But if we aren't aware of ourselves, we don't know our minds and so we follow after these things. People say, "My mind is upset," "My mind is unhappy," "My mind is scattered." But that's not really true. The mind isn't anything; the defilements are. People think their minds aren't comfortable or happy, but actually the mind is the most comfortable and happy thing. When we experience the different unsatisfactory states, that is not the mind. Make note of this: when you are experiencing these things in the future, remember, "Ajahn Chah said, 'This is not the mind.'"

We are practicing to reach the mind—the "old" mind. This original mind is unconditioned. In it there is no good or bad, long or short, black or white. But we are not content to remain with this mind, because we don't look at and understand things clearly.

Dharma is beyond the habits of the ordinary mind. Before we have trained well, we may mistake wrong for right and right for wrong. So it's necessary to listen to teaching to gain understanding of Dharma and be able to recognize Dharma in our own mind. Foolishness is in the mind. Intelligence is in the mind. Darkness and delusion exist in the mind. Knowledge and illumination exist in the mind.

It's like a dirty plate in your home that's filthy with grime and grease, or a dirty floor. Using soap and water to wash it, you can remove the dirt. When the dirt is gone, you have a clean plate or a clean floor. Here, the thing that is soiled is the mind. When we practice correctly, a clean thing is found, just like with the dirty floor that is made clean. When the dirt is scrubbed off, the condition of being clean appears. It's only the dirt that obscures it.

The mind in its natural state, the true mind, is something that is stable and undefiled. It is bright and clean. It becomes obscured and defiled because it meets with sense objects and comes under their influence through liking and disliking. It's not that the mind is inherently defiled, but that it is not yet established in Dharma, so phenomena can stain it.

The nature of the original mind is unwavering. It is tranquil. We are not tranquil because we are excited over sense objects, and we end up as slaves to the changing mental states that result. So, practice really means searching to find our way back to the original state, the "old thing." It is finding our old home, the original mind that does not waver and change following various phenomena. It is by nature perfectly peaceful; it is something that is already within us.

2

Understanding Phenomena

THE CAUSES FOR NOT being peaceful are within us. They manifest when we are deluded by internal and external phenomena. What we have to do is train the mind in correct view. We don't see correctly, so we are going a different way, and we are thus experiencing everything as too short, too long, too something. "Correct" means seeing the characteristics of impermanence, unsatisfactoriness, and lack of a self in all we experience, meaning our bodies and minds.

All things just as they are display the truth. But we have biases and preferences about how we want them to be. We are practicing to become like the Buddha, the "knower of the world," and the world is these phenomena abiding as they are.

When objects of mind arise, whether internally or externally, those are what we call sense phenomena or mental activity. The one who is aware of phenomena is called—well, whatever you want to call it is OK; you can call it "mind." The phenomenon is one thing, and the one who knows it is another. It's like the eye and the forms it sees. The eye isn't the objects, and the objects aren't the eye. The ear hears sounds, but the ear isn't the sound and the sound isn't the ear. When there is contact between the two, then things happen.

Our attitude toward these five *khandha*s (the "aggregates of existence," body, sensations, perceptions, thoughts, and consciousness), these heaps that we see right here, should be one of dispassion and detachment, because they don't follow our wishes. I think that's probably enough. If they survive, we shouldn't be overly joyful to the point of forgetting ourselves. If they break up, we shouldn't be overly dejected by that. Recognizing this much should be enough.

Whether we are undertaking insight meditation or tranquillity meditation, just this is what it's really about. But nowadays, it seems to me that when Buddhists talk about these things according to the traditional explanations, it becomes vague and mixed up. But the truth isn't vague or mixed up. It remains as it is. So I feel it's better to seek out the source, looking at the way things originate in the mind. There's not a lot to this.

It is said, "This world of beings, ruled by aging and impermanence, is not long-lasting." "Beings" means us. We are called human beings. There are beings different from us, such as animal beings, cattle and fowl, for example. But for all of them, aging is a fact of their existence, the decay of the various constituents of their physical bodies. These things are always changing. They don't have freedom to remain, but must follow the way of *sankhara,* conditioned phenomena. The world of beings is thus, and we find ourselves always dissatisfied. Our emotions of love and hate never bring us satisfaction. We never feel we have enough, but are always somehow obstructed. Simply speaking, as we say in our local idiom, we are people who don't know enough; we aren't satisfied to be what we are. So our minds waver endlessly, always changing into good and bad states with the different phenomena we encounter, like a cow not satisfied with its own tail. With unstable minds, we are always in this unsatisfied state, no matter what we experience. We become slaves to desire.

Being a slave is a state of great suffering. A slave must always obey the master, even when told to do something that might get him killed. But with our craving, we are always eager and willing to follow its orders. Because of our self-cherishing habits, we are thus ruled.

This world of beings actually has no ruler. It is we ourselves who rule our own lives, because we have the power to decide on doing good or doing evil. No one else does these for us.

This world of beings has nothing of its own. Nothing belongs to anyone. Seeing this with correct view, we will release our grip, just letting things be. Coming into this world and realizing its limitations, we do our business; we seek a profit in the way of building *parami*s, the spiritual perfections.

3

That's About Right

WHERE IS THE DHARMA? The entire Dharma is sitting here with us. Whatever you experience is right, just as it is. When you've gotten old, don't think that's something wrong. When your back is aching, don't think that's some kind of mistake. If you are suffering, don't think that's wrong. If you're happy, don't think that's wrong.

All of this is Dharma. Suffering is merely suffering. Happiness is merely happiness. Hot is merely hot. Cold is merely cold. It's not that "I am happy, I am suffering, I am good, I am bad, I gained something, I lost something." What is there that can be lost by a person? There's nothing at all. Gaining something is Dharma. Losing it is Dharma. Being happy and comfortable is Dharma. Being ill at ease is Dharma. It means not grasping onto all these conditions, but recognizing what they are. If you have happiness, you realize, "Oh! Happiness is not permanent." If you are suffering, you realize, "Oh! Suffering is not permanent." "Oh, this is really good!"—that's not permanent. "That is bad, really bad!"—not permanent. They have their limits, so don't hold so firmly onto them.

The Buddha taught about impermanence. This is the way things are—they don't follow anyone's wishes. That is noble truth. Impermanence rules the world, and that is something permanent. This is the point we are deluded at, so this is where you should be looking. Whatever occurs, recognize it as right. Everything is right in its own nature, which is ceaseless motion and change. Our bodies exist thus. All phenomena of body and mind exist thus. We can't stop them; they can't be stilled. Not being stilled means their nature of impermanence. If we don't struggle with this reality, then wherever we are, we will be happy. Wherever we sit, we are happy. Wherever we sleep, we are happy. Even when we get old, we won't make a big deal out of it. You stand up and your back hurts, and you think, "Yeah, that's about right." It's right, so don't fight it. When the pain stops, you might think, "Ah, that's better!" But it's not better. You're still alive, so it will hurt again. This is the way it is, so you have to keep turning your mind to this contemplation and not let it back away from the practice. Keep steadily at it, and don't trust in things too much; trust the Dharma instead, that life is like this. Don't believe in happiness. Don't believe in suffering. Don't get stuck in following after anything.

With this kind of foundation, then whatever occurs, never mind—it isn't anything permanent, it isn't anything certain. The world is like this. Then there is a path for us, a path to manage our lives and protect ourselves. With mindfulness and clear awareness of ourselves, with all-encompassing wisdom, that is the path in harmony. Nothing can deceive us, because we have entered the path. Constantly looking here, we are meeting the Dharma at all times.

4

Seeing Things Through

Ajahn Chah's Practice

AJAHN CHAH HAD A quality of boldness in his practice. He didn't shrink from whatever troubled him. Afraid of ghosts (extremely common in Thailand), he went to spend the night in a charnel ground, where he had such terrifying experiences that the next morning he passed blood in his urine, but the following night he stayed there again.

He was frank about his weaknesses. Sexual desire was a great problem for him when he was a young monk. "When I practiced alone in the forest, sometimes I'd see monkeys in the trees and I'd feel desire. I'd sit there and look and think, and I'd have lust: 'It wouldn't be bad to go and be a monkey with them!' This is what sexual desire can do—even a monkey could get me aroused."

Tormented by lust, Ajahn Chah did walking meditation with his robe hitched up above his waist. He had visions of female genitalia everywhere, but he didn't succumb; rather, he thought that it must be the residue from past lives of consorting with the opposite sex and that he was making an end of it in this life. He would see things through, with the attitude that there was no other place and no other time to do it, and he often said that he was able to develop wisdom precisely because of his great store of defilements.

5

Buddhas and Bodhisattvas

You could say we are sentient beings working to become awakening beings, bodhisattvas. This is just the same as the Lord Buddha did.

When the mind is obscured by desire, aversion, and delusion, that is a sentient being. But whenever we have the *brahmavihara,* the "divine abidings" of loving kindness, compassion, empathetic joy, and equanimity established in our hearts, then we can be called excellent beings, or we could also be called bodhisattvas. Even beings without such qualities can develop them and eventually become enlightened. In the past, the one who was to become the Lord Buddha was also merely a human being. But he developed himself to be an extraordinary being, one who was suffused with the brahmaviharas, and thus he was called the Bodhisattva. Then through his persistent contemplation to know the truth, to know the facts of impermanence, suffering, and lack of a self, he attained to full knowledge and was awakened as the Buddha. So don't get the idea that there was only one Buddha. The one Buddha is actually the *saccadhamma,* the truth, and whoever is awakened to that is

Buddha. There may be hundreds or thousands of buddhas, but they will all follow in this same track, that of correct view.

Yes, there is one Buddha, meaning right view. Whoever awakens to that is not different from the Buddha. So the Buddha and sentient beings are not far apart. This is something to be realized within. Realizing the truth of original mind, we will see that it is impossible to describe or give to another. There is no way to show it, nothing to compare it to. It is beyond speech or concept. Teaching others, we rely on externals to transmit ideas, but realization of the truth must be accomplished by each individual.

6

—

Seeing Things as They Really Are

THE BUDDHA TAUGHT TO look at whatever appears. Things don't stay. Having arisen, they cease. Ceasing, they appear again, and having appeared, they cease. But a confused, uninstructed person doesn't want it to be this way. If we meditate and become tranquil, we want to remain like that and don't want any disturbance. But that isn't realistic. The Buddha wanted us to first look at the facts and know these things as deceptive; then we can really have tranquillity. When we don't know them, we become their owners, and the trap of self-view comes about. So we have to go back to the origin and find out how it happened that way. We have to understand the way things really are, the way things contact the mind and how the mind reacts, and then we can be at peace. This is what we have to investigate. If we don't want things to happen the way they do, we won't have peace. Wherever we may try to escape to, things still happen the same way; this is their nature.

Simply speaking, this is truth. Impermanence, suffering, and absence of a self are the nature of phenomena. They are nothing else but this, but we give things more meaning than they really have.

It's really not so difficult to make wisdom arise. It means looking for the causes and understanding the nature of things. When the mind is agitated, you should realize, "This is not certain. Impermanent!" When the mind is calm, don't start thinking, "Ah, really peaceful!" because that is also not certain.

When someone asks, "What kind of food do you like best?" don't get too serious about that. If you say you really like something, what's the big deal? Think about it—if you eat it every day, will you still like it so much? You'll probably get to the point where you say, "Oh, man, not again!"

Do you understand this? You can end up getting sick of the very thing you like. It's because of the changeability of things, and this is what you should come to know. Pleasure is uncertain. Unhappiness is uncertain. Liking is uncertain. Tranquillity is uncertain. Agitation is uncertain. Absolutely everything is uncertain. So whatever occurs, we understand this, and we won't be taken in by anything. All experiences without exception are uncertain, because impermanence is their nature. Impermanence means that things are not fixed or stable, and very simply speaking, this truth is the Buddha.

Anicca, uncertainty, is the truth. Truth is present for us to see, but we don't take a good, clear look at it. The Buddha said, "Those who see the Dharma see me." If we see anicca, that quality of being uncertain, in all things, then detachment and world-weariness come about: "Oh! This is merely so much. Eh! That is merely so much. It is not actually anything so great, it is merely so much." The mind becomes firm in this: "It is merely that much. Aha!" After realizing this, we needn't do anything very difficult in our contemplation. Whatever we encounter, the mind is saying, "It's merely that much," and it stops. That's the end of it. We will realize that all phenomena are only deceptions; nothing is stable or permanent, but rather everything is ceaselessly changing and has the characteristics of impermanence, suffering, and not-self. It's like a blazing red-hot iron ball that has been heated in a furnace. What part of it will be cool? Try to touch it if you will. Touch the top and it will be hot. Touch the bottom and it will be hot. Touch the sides and they will be hot. Why is it hot? It is a blazing iron ball that is red-hot throughout. When we understand this, we won't touch it. When you are feeling, "This is really good! I like it! Let me have it!" don't give such thoughts credence; don't take them too seriously. It's a red-hot iron ball. If you touch any part of it, if you try to pick it up, you will be burned, you will experience a lot of pain, your skin will break open and bleed.

We should be contemplating this at all times, walking, standing, sitting, lying down. Even when we are in the toilet, when we are going somewhere, when we are eating, or after we have eaten and we excrete the waste from our food, we should be seeing that all we experience is unstable and impermanent, and that it is also unsatisfactory and without self. Things that are unstable and impermanent are uncertain and unreal. Without exception, they are all untrue. It's just like the red-hot iron ball—where can we touch it that it won't be hot? Absolutely every part of it is hot, so we stop trying to touch it.

This is not something difficult to train in. For example, parents warn a child not to play with fire: "Don't go near the fire! It's dangerous! You'll get burned!" The child may not believe her parents or understand what they are talking about. But if she touches the fire just once and gets a burn, after that the parents won't need to explain anything or try to control her.

No matter how much the mind is attracted to or infatuated by anything, you have to keep reminding it, "It's not sure! It's not permanent!" You might get something, like a glass, and start thinking how beautiful it is. "What a nice glass. I will store it away and take really good care of it so it doesn't get broken." Then you have to tell yourself, "It's not certain." You could be drinking from it and set it down by your elbow, and in a moment of carelessness you knock it over and it breaks.

If it doesn't break today, it will break tomorrow. If it doesn't break tomorrow, it will break the day after tomorrow. Things that are subject to being broken are not where you should be placing your trust.

This impermanence is the real Dharma. Things are not stable or real. Nothing about them is real, and just this fact is what is real. Are you going to argue this point? It is the most certain thing: being born, you must age, fall ill, and die. This is the permanent and certain reality, and this permanent truth is born of the truth of impermanence. Examining things thoroughly with the standard of "not permanent, not certain," a transformation takes place into something permanent and certain, and then one no longer carries the burden of things.

The disciples of the Buddha awakened to the truth of impermanence. From awakening to impermanence, they experienced detachment and weariness with things, or *nibbida.* This weariness is not aversion. If there is aversion, that is not really weariness, and it does not become a path. Nibbida is not what we think of as world-weariness in the ordinary way. For example, living with our families, when we are not getting along well, we might start thinking that we're really becoming disenchanted in the way the teachings mention. That's not it; that's merely our defilements increasing and oppressing our hearts. "I'm really fed up—I'm going to leave it all behind!" This is weariness because of defilement, and what really happens is that your defilements become greater than before you gave yourself this idea of weariness over things that disagree with you.

It's like the idea we have of *metta,* loving kindness. We think we are supposed to have loving kindness toward people and all living things. So we tell ourselves, "I shouldn't have anger toward them. I should feel compassion. Really, sentient beings are lovable." You start having affection for them, and it ends up being desire and attachment. Be careful about this! It's not just a matter of what we normally call love. This is not metta in the way of Dharma. It is metta mixed with selfishness. We want something from others, and we call it metta. This is similar to our ordinary "world-weariness." "Oh yeah, I'm really tired of it all, I'm getting out!" That's just big defilement. It's not world-weariness or dispassion; it's only giving the same name to it. That's not the way of the Buddha. If it is correct, there is giving up, without aversion or aggression, without any harmfulness toward anyone. One is not complaining or finding fault—one just sees everything as empty.

It means coming to the point where the mind is empty. It is empty of grasping attachment to things. This doesn't mean that there is nothing, no people or objects in the world. There is empty mind, there are people, there are things. But in the mind there is the perception of it all as truth, as something uncertain. Things are seen as being the way they are, following their natural course as elemental nature arising and passing away.

For example, you might have a vase. You feel that it's something nice, but from its own side it exists indifferently. It doesn't have anything to say; it is only you who have the feelings about it, you who live and die over it. If you dislike or hate it, it won't be affected. That's your affair. It is indifferent, but you have these feelings of like or dislike and then get attached to them. We judge different things as being good or bad. This "good" troubles our hearts. "Bad" troubles our hearts. Both are defilements.

We don't need to run away to any other place; we need only look at and investigate this point. This is the way the mind is. When we dislike something, that object of dislike isn't affected; it remains as it is. When we like something, it isn't affected by our liking, but remains just as it is. We are only making ourselves insane, that's all.

You think some things are good, you see other things as great, but you are projecting these ideas from yourself. If you are aware of yourself, you will realize that all these things are equal.

An easy illustration is food. We feel this or that kind of food is nice. When we see the dishes on the table, they are attractive; once everything is put together in the stomach, it's another story. But we look at the different dishes and say, "This one's for me. That one's yours. That one is hers." When we've eaten and then it comes out the other end, probably no one is going to contend over it and say,

"This is mine. That's yours." Or is that not so? Will you still be possessive and greedy over it?

This is putting it briefly and simply. If you see clearly and make up your mind, everything will be of equal value to you. When we have desires and think in terms of "mine" and "yours," then we end up in conflict. When we see things as being equal, then we don't see them as belonging to anyone—they are just conditions existing as they are. No matter how fine the food is that we eat, once it is excreted, no one wants to pick it up and make a big deal out of it. No one will fight over it.

When we realize things as this one dharma, all being of the same nature, we relax our grip, we put things down. We see they are empty, and we don't have love and hate for them; we have peace. It is said, "Nirvana is the supreme happiness; nirvana is the supreme emptiness."

Please listen to this carefully. Happiness in the world is not supreme, ultimate happiness. What we conceive of as emptiness is not supreme emptiness. If it is supreme emptiness, there is an end of grasping and attachment. If it is supreme happiness, there is peace. But the peace we know is still not supreme. The happiness we know is not supreme. If we reach nirvana, then emptiness is supreme. Happiness is supreme. There is a transformation. The character of happiness is transformed into peace. There is happiness, but we don't give it any special meaning. There is suffering also. When these occur, we see them as equal. Their value is the same.

The sensory experiences we like and dislike are equal. But when they contact us, we don't see them as equal. If something is pleasing, we are really happy over it. If something is displeasing, we want to destroy it. So they aren't the same to us, but in truth they really are equal. We have to train in this: they are equal in that they are unstable and impermanent.

It's like the example of food. We say this kind of food is good, that dish is great, that other one is wonderful. But when they end up together inside the body and then get excreted, it's all the same.

Then you won't hear anyone complain, "How come I got so little?" At that point our minds don't get carried away over it.

If we don't experience the truth of impermanence, unsatisfactoriness, and not-self, then there is no end to suffering. If we pay attention, we can see it every moment. It is present in mind and body, and we can see it. This is where we find peace.

7

That's Good Too

Ajahn Chah's View

WHEN WESTERNERS STARTED ARRIVING at Wat Pah Pong, American monk Sumedho Bhikkhu was their translator and adviser. After a couple of years, Sumedho took off for India. Then a young American monk in his second year of study with Ajahn Chah inherited the job of translator. One day some Mormons from the U.S. Air Force base in Ubon came to request a talk on Buddhism in their chapel, and the task fell to the young translator.

On the afternoon of the talk, Ajahn Chah, who was to go along, but for some reason hadn't offered to speak, was bucking up the monk. "Have you heard of the 'doctor of necessity?'" he asked. The monk said that he hadn't.

Ajahn Chah continued. "There's the genuine doctor, and there's the doctor of necessity. The genuine doctor went to medical school and is fully trained to do everything a doctor should do. But when there's no such doctor around, like in the villages here, someone has to fill in. He can give an injection, clean a cut, or hand out pills—that's about all. That's the doctor of necessity."

So the monk gave the lecture his best shot, and the monks who accompanied him pitched in and helped answer questions. Back in the monastery that night, as he did walking meditation, the words of his talk kept running through his head. The next day he mentioned this to Ajahn Chah. "My talk was going on all night!" he told him.

Ajahn Chah laughed, and said, "Well, that's good too [one of his favorite phrases]. It's letting you see impermanence, unsatisfactoriness, and not-self."

8

The Buddha's Inspiration

THERE IS DARK, AND there is light; there is hot, and there is cold; there is birth and death, and there must be a state beyond birth and death: the Buddha, before his enlightenment, reasoned and inferred in this way. Not seeking to know a lot of things, he just considered this much. He practiced according to this view, with real enthusiasm. He didn't take shortcuts.

The Buddha practiced intently, without retreating, because he had this certainty in his mind, that there being darkness, there must be illumination. When there is pleasure and happiness, there must be pain and suffering. There is heat, and there must be coolness to relieve it. There is birth, and there most surely must be non-birth to cure it. Of this he was certain. No one told him this; it was his state of mind and temperament occurring due to the past conditions of his spiritual perfections.

So having this view of things, he left home to practice for six years. He was undeterred and did not slacken his efforts, being unconcerned with fatigue and hardship. He wanted to retrace to the source: "Where do things come from? What is suffering born of?"

He kept on investigating continuously, until he realized that it comes from birth. We suffer because we were born.

What does birth come from? It comes from attachment. He just aimed his attention at this, grasping attachment. Birth, aging, illness, death, suffering, sorrow, despair, grief, and lamentation follow from it. This is the cycle.

There is birth, and birth is the cause for the various sufferings to come about. So, if there is birth, is there a place of non-birth? He considered this further, and concluded that there really ought to be: There is heat, and there is cold; there is happiness, and there is suffering; so there being happiness and suffering, there must be a place beyond happiness or suffering. There is the realm of birth and death, so there unquestionably must be the birthless and deathless. He became convinced of this and was determined to realize it. Finally he realized that knowing there is suffering, knowing the cause of suffering, knowing the cessation of suffering, and knowing the path to the cessation of suffering is the way of the awakened being, the *ariya*. It is not necessary to know a lot of things; just this is what needs to be known. This is the path, the way for all of us to follow. A practitioner needn't seek other knowledge.

9

Keep Some Perspective

ONE DAY A HOG farmer came to see me. He was complaining about business. "Oh man, this year it's really too much! The price of feed is up. The price of pork is down. I'm losing my shirt!"

I listened to his laments, then I said, "Don't feel too sorry for yourself, sir. If you were a pig, then you'd have good reason to feel sorry for yourself. When the price of pork is high, the pigs are slaughtered. When the price of pork is low, the pigs are still slaughtered. The pigs really have something to complain about. The people shouldn't be complaining. Think about this seriously, please."

He was only worried about the prices he was getting. The pigs have a lot more to worry about, but we don't consider that. We're not being killed, so we can still try to find a way to get by.

10

The Buddha's Search

WHEN THE BUDDHA SET out in search of liberation, he sought out the famous teachers of that time. First he went to the hermit Alara. He saw him and his disciples sitting in *samadhi,* meditative concentration, and thought that might bring peace. He observed how they sat cross-legged, with body erect and eyes closed. He had never seen such a thing, and it was impressive to him. He requested to stay there and studied and practiced diligently, meditating on the breath. But he came to realize one important fact, that it was not a way to escape from suffering. Why? Because he looked at his mind and saw that when he released it from the state of samadhi, it would start thinking and wandering, and he realized there was still something remaining; it would go to create things here and there. So he realized there was more to do. Having stayed with that teacher for some time, he continued on in his search. Yes, it was one kind of path, but not a path leading out of suffering, because the mind still retained its grasping attachments.

He went on to meet his next teacher, Udaka, and practiced the eight meditative absorptions, reaching the "plane of nothing at all," an extremely subtle state of mind. He could remain in this peaceful samadhi for a long time, but again came to realize it wasn't the correct path, because when he returned to his ordinary state, the mind went back to its old habits, carrying its old burdens.

This was still the level of samadhi; this is the nature of samadhi. No matter how refined the mind could become, there being refinement meant there was also coarseness. So insight started to come about here: one could attain these extremely refined and subtle states, but having delight in this refinement created the possibility for coarseness to come about.

The Buddha looked deeper, and he saw that if the subtle still remains, the Conqueror (*Jinasava;* lit. "the one who has realized the ending of the taints") does not come to be. There can be no end of things. If there is birth, then there will be illness, aging, and death without end; and he saw that grasping is the cause of this. He investigated to see clearly, to the point where he became disenchanted and turned away. He saw that he had been playing with these things for countless lifetimes in all sorts of states, and thus he was still in this condition of dissatisfaction. Trying to get to the end, to get enough, could never be accomplished. Even if he were to gain all the wealth and enjoyment in the world, he would still have suffering. He was certain of this now. He saw impermanence, suffering, and absence of a self in his mind. He saw that all phenomena appear and then cease to be.

So as he continued practicing, he became more certain about this. He attained the eight *jhana*s, the meditative absorptions, but still wisdom had not been born. If there were wisdom, it would have to be the state of insight (*vipassana*), meaning knowing according to the truth and letting go—letting go of coarse and refined.

To reach the place where there was no more coarse or refined remaining—what should he do? How should he practice? He kept on investigating. He looked at all objects of mind, all phenomena contacting the mind, and saw that they are impermanent (anicca), suffering (dukkha), and not-self (anatta), these three characteristics.

This is the meditation object of vipassana. This is what enables the mind to see things as they really are.

Realizing this, then when phenomena appeared, he didn't pursue them. He remained unshakable, taking the measure of things like this. He realized the three characteristics as the way of vipassana, and when anything contacted his mind, he measured it according to this. He knew things for what they were, so he didn't hold them, and practicing like this became the cause for not having grasping.

PART TWO

ANICCA

Impermanence

11

Bringing the Mind under Our Command

WHATEVER STATES OF MIND, happy or unhappy, occur, never mind—we should constantly be reminding ourselves, "This is uncertain."

This is something people don't consider very much, that "this is uncertain." Just this is the vital factor that will bring about wisdom. In order to cease our coming and going and find rest, we only need to say, "This is uncertain." Sometimes we may be distraught over something to the point that tears are flowing; that is something not certain. When moods of desire or aversion come to us, we should just remind ourselves of this one thing. Whether standing, walking, sitting, or lying down, whatever appears is uncertain. Can't you do this? Keep it up no matter what happens. Give it a try. You don't need a lot—just this will work. This is something that brings wisdom.

The way I practice meditation is not very complicated—just this. This is what it all comes down to: "It's uncertain." Everything meets at this point.

You don't need to keep track of all the various instances of mental experience. When you sit in meditation, there may be various conditions of mind appearing, seeing and knowing all manner of things, experiencing different states. Don't keep track of them, and don't get wrapped up in them. You only need to remind yourself that they're uncertain. That's enough. That's simple, and it's easy to do. Then you can stop. Knowledge will come, but then don't make too much out of that or get attached to it.

This understanding of things is always timely and relevant. At all times, it is impermanence that rules. This is something you should meditate on.

The true and correct words of the sages will not lack mention of impermanence. If there is no mention of impermanence, it is not the speech of the wise. It is not the speech of the enlightened ones; it's called speech that does not accept the truth of existence.

As I see it, once we have correct knowledge, the mind comes under our command. What is this command about? The command is in anicca, knowing that everything is impermanent. Everything stops here when we see clearly, and it becomes the cause for us letting go. Then we let things be, according to their nature. If nothing is occurring, we abide in equanimity, and if something comes up, we contemplate: Does it cause us to have suffering? Do we hold onto it with grasping attachment? Is there anything there? This is what supports and sustains our practice. If we practice and get to this point, I think every one of us will realize genuine peace. If we reach this place of recognizing truth, we will be uncomplicated, undemanding people, content with what we have, easy to speak to and unassuming in our actions. Without difficulty or trouble, we will live at ease. One who meditates and realizes a tranquil mind will be like this.

12

A Lot of Defilements

Ajahn Chah at Play

AJAHN CHAH SPOKE REPEATEDLY of uncertainty, and he also made sure that the life in his monasteries reflected that truth of existence. Disciples learned to live without attachment to routines, expectations, possessions, even to him.

In later years, as Ajahn Chah's pace became slower, he would go for almsround to the village nearest the monastery. Usually when the line of monks got to the end of the village, when the last donors had offered their rice, a novice or junior monk would relieve him of his bowl, and most of the entourage would walk on ahead, bowing their heads slightly and putting their palms together in a gesture of respect as they went by him. Often he was accompanied by one of the older monks, but occasionally he walked alone. Sometimes as you ducked your head to pass, he would call your name, so you would fall in step behind him.

One such morning he began to question me about the abbots I had stayed with in the branch monasteries. When we started talking about Ajahn Sinuan, a senior disciple who was now abbot of his own monastery and who was one of Ajahn Chah's favorite whipping boys, I said that I had eventually come to feel that Ajahn Sinuan was somewhat lazy and liked to goof off, in spite of his protestations about what an ardent practitioner he was.

"Right," said Ajahn Chah. "Just like me. . . . I've got a lot of defilements. I like to fool around."

Although I realized he was putting me on, I was startled to hear such talk and didn't know what to say. Ajahn Chah went on, bending his head toward me, lowering his voice, and speaking in mock confidentiality. "Listen: I'm planning to disrobe, and I want you to help me find a nice woman."

13

It's Not Permanent, It's Not Sure

WE FOCUS ON THE here and now Dharma. This is where we can let go of things and resolve our difficulties. Right now, in the present, because the present moment contains both cause and result. The present is the fruit of the past. It is also the cause of the future. That we are sitting here right now is the result of what we have done in the past, and what we do now will become the cause for what we experience in the future. So the Buddha taught to discard the past and discard the future. Saying *discard* doesn't really mean that we throw anything away, but that we remain in this single point of the present, where the past and future come together. So the word *discard* is just a way of speaking; what we want to do is be aware of the present, where causes and results are to be found. We look at the present and see continuous arising and ceasing, arising and ceasing.

I keep saying this, but people don't really take it to heart: phenomena appear in the present moment, and they are not stable or reliable. People don't look into this very much. Whatever comes about, I will say, "Oh! This is not permanent," or, "This is uncertain." This is extremely simple. Whatever occurs is impermanent and uncertain. But not seeing or understanding this, we become confused and distressed. In what is impermanent we see permanence. In what is uncertain we see certainty. I explain it but people don't get it, and they end up living their lives in endless pursuit of things.

Really, if you reach the point of peace, you will be here at this place I am talking about, this point in the present. Whatever appears, any form of happiness or suffering, you will see that it is uncertain. This very uncertainty is itself the Buddha, because uncertainty is the Dharma, and the Dharma is the Buddha. But most people believe the Buddha and the Dharma to be something external to themselves.

When the mind starts to realize that all things without exception are by their very nature uncertain, the problems of grasping and attachment start to decrease and wither away. If we understand this, the mind starts to let go and put things down, not grasping onto things, and attachment can come to an end. When it comes to an end, one must reach the Dharma; there is nothing beyond this.

When we meditate, this is what we want to realize. We want to see impermanence, unsatisfactoriness, and not-self, and this begins with seeing uncertainty. When we see it perfectly clearly, then we can let go. When we experience happiness, we see that "this is uncertain." When we experience suffering, we see that "this is uncertain." We get the idea that it would be good to go to some place, and we realize, "It's uncertain." We think it would be good to stay where we are, and we realize, "This is uncertain, too." We see that absolutely everything is uncertain, and we will live at ease. Then we can stay where we are and be comfortable, or we can go somewhere else and be comfortable.

Doubts will end like this. They will end by this method of practicing in the present. There's no need to be anxious about the past, because it has gone. Whatever happened in the past has arisen and ceased in the past, and now it is finished. We can let go of concern about the future, because whatever will occur in the future will occur and cease in the future.

When the lay supporters come to make offerings here, they recite, "In the end, may we finally reach nirvana in a future time." When or where that is they don't really know. It's so very far away. They don't say, "Here and now." They say, "Sometime in the future." It's always somewhere, sometime "there." Not "here." Only "there." In the next life it will also be "there," and in future lives it will be "there." So they never arrive, because it's always "there."

It's like people inviting an old monk to receive almsfood in a village and saying, "Please, venerable sir, go for alms in the village over there." Then when he has walked to a distant village, they say, "Please, venerable one, receive your alms over there." He keeps on walking, but wherever he arrives, they tell him, "Please receive your almsfood over there." The poor old fellow will never see a morsel of food; he just keeps on walking "there," and "over there," and nothing comes of it.

We tend to be like this. We never say "here and now." Why not? Is there something wrong with the present? It's because we are still involved with things. We still delight in the worldly and don't dare to give it up. So we prefer to let it be "sometime in the future." Just like someone egging on the old monk with talk of a meal offering: "Please, sir, travel over there for your alms." So he goes on in search of the place "over there" where he can find alsm-food to sustain himself, but it's never "here," and he never receives any food.

Let's talk about here and now, in the present. Practice really can be done in the present; we don't need to look to sometime in the future. Rather than becoming anxious about anything, we just look at the here and now Dharma and see uncertainty and impermanence. Then Buddha Mind, the One Who Knows, comes to be. It is developed through this knowledge that all things are impermanent.

This is where knowledge is gained. Samadhi, the collectedness of the mind, can be developed here. There is the peace of living in the forest: there is calm when the eye doesn't see and the ear doesn't hear. The mind is pacified of seeing and hearing. But it is not pacified of the defilements. The defilements are still there, but at that time they aren't appearing. It's like water with sediment in it: when it is still, it's clear, but when something stirs it, the dirt rises up and clouds it. You are the same in your practice. When you see forms, hear sounds, have disagreeable experiences, or have bodily sensations that are unpleasant, then you are disturbed. If these don't occur, you are comfortable; you are comfortable with the defilements.

You might want to get something, like a camera. If you get one, you feel happy. Until you have it you won't be satisfied, and finally when you are able to get it there is some pleasure in that. Then if it's stolen, you will be upset. Your happiness has gone. So before you can get what you want, there is unhappiness; when you get it, there is happiness; and then when it's gone, there is unhappiness again.

The samadhi that comes from living in a peaceful environment is like that. There is happiness in being pleased by the tranquil state, but the happiness only goes so far, because the mind is under the influence of desire for something that is changeable. After a while it will be gone, and unhappiness will take its place—just as when a thief gets your camera. This is the peace of samadhi, the temporary peace of tranquillity meditation.

We have to look into this a little more deeply. Whatever we have will become a source of suffering when we lose it if we aren't aware of its impermanence. If we are aware of it, then we can make use of things without being burdened by them.

You might want to do business, and you need to get a loan from a bank. If you can't get it in spite of all your efforts, you will have some suffering. Finally the bank might agree to lend you money, and you are delighted. Your delight won't last for too many hours—but the interest will start piling up. After a while, that will become your concern: whatever you are doing, even just sitting back in your armchair, they will be charging you interest. So there is suffering over this. Before, there was suffering over not being able to find a loan. When you got one, it seemed you'd be all set and everything would be OK, but then you had to start thinking about the interest on the loan, and suffering returned.

Thus, the Buddha taught to look in the present and see the impermanence of body and mind, of all phenomena as they appear and cease, without grasping at any of it. If we can do this, we will experience peace. This peace comes because of letting go; letting go comes about because of wisdom, the wisdom that comes from contemplation of impermanence, suffering, and not-self, the truth of experience, and witnessing this truth in one's own mind.

Practicing like this, we are continuously seeing clearly within our own minds. Phenomena arise and cease. Ceasing, there is new arising; arising, there is ceasing. If we form attachment to what occurs, suffering comes about right there. If we are letting go, suffering will not come about. We see this in our own minds.

We can gain real certainty about the Dharma when meditating like this, and we can come to the point where all we have to do is be looking at our minds in the present. We let go of the past and the future and look in the present, and we see the three characteristics continuously and in everything. Walking, there is impermanence. Standing, there is impermanence. Sitting, there is impermanence. That's the inherent truth in things. If you are looking for certainty or permanence, you can only find it in things being this way and not changing into some other way. When your view matures like this, you will be at peace.

Or do you think that by going to meditate on a lonely mountaintop you'll have peace? You may have peace for a while. But when the austerity of living there catches up with you, you'll start to feel hungry and exhausted. So you come down the mountain and head for town. Lots of good food and comforts there. But then you'll begin to think it's disturbing to your practice—better to go somewhere remote.

Really, someone who suffers when living alone is foolish. Someone who suffers when living with others is foolish. It's like chicken turds: if you carry them around by yourself, they stink. If you keep them when you're among others, they also stink. You carry the rotten things with you.

If we are astute, then we may be living around a lot of people and feel it isn't a peaceful environment, and that will be correct to some extent, but still it can be a cause for gaining wisdom. I developed some wisdom from having a lot of disciples. Laypeople came in large numbers, many monks came wanting to be disciples, and everyone had their own views and dispositions. I experienced a lot of different things, and I had to rise to the occasion. My capacity for patience and endurance was strengthened. To the extent that I could bear with it, I was able to keep practicing. Then all my experience became meaningful. But if we don't understand correctly, there is no resolution. Living alone will be good—until we get fed up with it. Then we'll think it's better to live in a group. Having simple food will seem good, and then maybe having a lot of food will seem to be the right way. It goes on like this when we can't resolve our minds once and for all.

Seeing that everything is unreliable, we will take all situations of lack or plenty as uncertain and not have attachment to them. We pay attention to the present moment, wherever this body happens to be dwelling. Then staying will be OK. Traveling will be OK. Everything will be OK, because we are focused on the practice of recognizing the way things really are.

People say, "Ajahn Chah only talks about 'not certain.'" They get fed up with hearing this, and they run away from me. "We went to listen to Ajahn Chah teach, but all he talked about was 'not certain.'" They can't bear to hear the same old thing anymore, so they leave. I guess they're going to look for some place where things will be certain. But they'll come back.

14

A Fish Story

AFTER I ORDAINED IN the Buddha's way, I started practicing, studying and then practicing, and faith came about. I would think about the lives of beings in the world. It all seemed very heartrending and pitiful. What was so pitiful about it? All the rich people would soon die and have to leave their big houses behind, leaving the children and grandchildren to fight over the estate. When I saw such things happening, it got to me. It made me feel pity toward rich and poor alike, toward the wise and the foolish—everyone living in this world was in the same boat.

Reflecting on our own mortality, about the condition of the world and the lives of sentient beings, brings about detachment and dispassion. The Dharma caused such feelings to fill my heart, waking me. Whatever situations I met, I was awake and alert. It means I was beginning to have some knowledge of Dharma. My mind was illumined, and I realized many things. I experienced bliss, a real satisfaction and delight in my way of life.

To put it simply, I felt I was different from others. I was a fully grown, normal man, but I could live the simple life of a monk in the forest. I didn't have any regrets or see any loss in it. When I saw others with their worldly involvements, I thought that was truly regrettable. I came to have real faith and trust in the path of practice I had chosen, and this faith has supported me right up to the present.

Now, in many places, the Buddha's way, meaning the genuine and direct teaching that instructs people to be honest and upright, to have loving kindness toward each other, seems to have been lost, and turmoil and distress are taking its place. People everywhere are making such great efforts in their lives, yet all they're doing is bringing suffering and difficulty on themselves. The Buddha teaches us to create benefit for ourselves and others in this life, as well as the ultimate benefit of spiritual welfare. We should do it now, in the present. We should be seeking out the knowledge that will help us do that, so that we can live our lives well, making good use of our resources, working with diligence in ways of right livelihood. Thinking about the meditative life, that we have taken up this way of life to dwell and practice in peace and simplicity, and developing a constant attitude of dispassion toward the shortcomings of the world, our practice will progress. Thinking constantly about the factors of practice, rapture comes about. The hairs of the body stand on end. There is a feeling of joy in reflecting on the way we live, in comparing our lives previously with our lives now.

⌒

I once taught a sage, years ago, when I was a young monk. He was a lay patron who came here to meditate and keep the eight precepts on the lunar observance days in the early years of Wat Pah Pong, but he still went fishing. I tried to teach him further but couldn't solve this problem. He said he didn't kill fish; they merely came to swallow his hook.

I kept at it, teaching him until he felt some contrition. He was ashamed of his fishing, but he kept doing it. Then his rationalization changed. He would put the hook in the water and announce,

"Whichever fish has reached the end of its karma to be alive, come eat my hook. If your time has not yet come, do not eat my hook." He had changed his excuse, but still the fish came to eat. Finally he started looking at them, their mouths caught on the hook, and he felt some pity. But he couldn't yet resolve his mind. "Well, I told them not to eat the hook if it wasn't time; what can I do if they still come?" And then he'd think, "But they are dying because of me!" He went back and forth on this until finally he could stop.

Then there were the frogs. He couldn't bear to stop catching frogs to eat. "Don't do this!" I told him. "Take a good look at them. If you can't stop killing them, then please just look at them first." So he picked up a frog and looked at it. He looked at its face, its eyes, its legs. "Oh man, it looks like my child! It has arms and legs. Its eyes are open. It's looking at me!" He felt hurt. But still he killed them. He looked at each one like this and then killed it, feeling he was doing something bad. His wife was pushing him, saying they wouldn't have anything to eat if he didn't kill them.

Finally he couldn't bear it anymore. He would catch them but wouldn't break their legs; previously he broke their legs so they couldn't hop away. Still, he couldn't make himself let them go. "Well, I'm just taking care of them, feeding them here. I'm only rearing them. Whatever someone else might do, I don't know about that." But of course he knew. The others were killing them for food. After a while he could admit this to himself. "Anyhow, I've cut my bad karma by 50 percent. Someone else does the killing."

This was starting to drive him crazy, but still he couldn't let go. He kept the frogs at home. He wouldn't break their legs anymore, but his wife would. "It's my fault. Even if I don't do it, she does it because of me." Finally he gave it up altogether. But then his wife was complaining. "What are we going to do? What should we eat?"

He was really caught now. When he came to the monastery, I lectured him on what he should do. When he returned home, his wife lectured him on what he should do. I was telling him to stop doing that, and his wife was pushing him to continue doing it. What to do? What a lot of suffering, he thought. Born into this world, we have to suffer like this.

In the end, his wife had to let go, too. So they stopped killing frogs. He worked in his field, tending his buffalo. Then he got the habit of releasing fish and frogs. When he saw fish caught in nets, he would set them free. One day when he was working, he went into a neighbor's house to get a drink of water. Nobody was home, but he heard the sound of something knocking. He was puzzled, but finally he saw what it was: there were some frogs in a pot and they were trying to escape. He looked around to make sure nobody was coming, and then he set them free.

After a while, his friend's wife came to prepare dinner. She opened the lid of the pot and saw the frogs were gone. She figured out what had happened. "It's that guy with the heart of merit."

The neighbor's wife managed to catch one frog, and she made a chili paste with it. They sat down to eat, and as he went to dip his ball of rice in the chili, she grabbed his wrist and said, "Hey! Heart of Merit! You shouldn't eat that! It's frog chili paste."

This was too much. What a lot of grief, just being alive and trying to feed oneself! Thinking about it, he couldn't see any way out. He was already an old man, so he decided to ordain.

He ordained in the local monastery, and after the ceremony he asked the preceptor what he should do. The preceptor told him, "If you're really doing this seriously, you ought to practice meditation. Follow a meditation master; don't stay here near the houses." He understood, and so he decided to do that. He slept one night in the temple and in the morning took his leave, asking where he could find Ajahn Tongrat, one of the famous masters of that time.

He shouldered his almsbowl and wandered off, a new monk who couldn't yet put on his robes very neatly. But he found his way to Ajahn Tongrat.

"Venerable Master, I have no other aim in life. I want to offer my body and my life to you."

Ajahn Tongrat replied, "Very good! Lots of merit! You almost missed me. I was just about to go on my way. So do your prostrations and take a seat there."

The new monk asked, "Now that I've ordained, what should I do?"

It happened that they were sitting by an old tree stump. Ajahn Tongrat pointed to it and said, "Make yourself like this tree stump. Don't do anything else, just make yourself like this tree stump." This was how he taught him to meditate.

So Ajahn Tongrat went on his way, and the monk stayed there to contemplate his words. "Ajahn taught to make myself like a tree stump. What am I supposed to do?" He pondered this continuously, whether walking, sitting, or lying down to sleep. He thought about how there was first a seed, how it grew into a tree, got bigger, and aged, and was finally cut down, just leaving a stump. Now that it was a stump, it wouldn't be growing anymore, and nothing would bloom from it. He kept on discussing this in his mind, considering it over and over, until it became his meditation object. He expanded it to apply to all things in the world, and then he was able to turn it inward and apply it to himself. "After a while, I am probably going to be like this stump, a useless thing."

Realizing this gave him the determination not to disrobe. When the mind is made up like this, there won't be anything that can stop it.

All of us share this condition. Please think about this and try to apply it to your practice. Being born as a human is full of difficulties. And it's not just that it's been difficult for us so far—in the future there will also be difficulty. Young people will grow up, grownups will age, aged ones will fall ill, ill people will die. It keeps on going like this, the cycle of ceaseless transformation that never comes to an end. So the Buddha taught us to meditate.

In meditation, first we have to practice samadhi, which means making the mind still and peaceful. Like water in a basin: if we keep putting things in it and stirring it up, it will always be murky. If the mind is always allowed to be thinking and worrying over things, we can never see anything clearly. But if we let the water in the basin settle and become still, then we can see all sorts of things reflected in it. When the mind is settled and still, wisdom will be able to see things. The illuminating light of wisdom surpasses any other kind of light.

15

A Perplexed Meditator Meets the Buddha

THERE WAS A VENERABLE elder in the time of the Buddha. He was a serious meditator. He wanted to get to the bottom of things, and so he went to practice samadhi in seclusion.

Sometimes his meditation was peaceful, and sometimes it wasn't. He couldn't make it stable. Sometimes he was lazy, and sometimes he felt diligent. So he started to have some doubts, and he thought he needed to learn more about the path of practice. He would hear of different teachers: "Such-and-such master is really good. His practice and teaching are excellent; his fame has spread far and wide." And he would seek out that teacher to learn his way of practice. After studying for a while, he would go back to practice on his own again.

Then, practicing what he had learned from that teacher, he found that some things agreed with his own ideas and some didn't. And his doubts would keep on coming. He would hear someone praising another teacher, and so he went to see that one. He would learn from that teacher and then end up comparing it with what he had heard from the previous one. He kept on learning and comparing, and the teachings didn't agree; and further, they didn't agree with his own ideas. So his doubts increased even more.

And then there were the methods of practicing samadhi. He thought about them all and tried them all, and it only made his mind scattered and disturbed—it didn't bring his mind to concentration. He was getting to the point of exhaustion and was still as full of doubts as ever.

One day he heard about the monk Gotama, that he was indeed someone special. He couldn't resist; off he went yet once again.

Arriving at the place where the Buddha was staying, he listened to the teaching of the Dharma. Gotama said, "Trying to gain understanding from another's words will not bring an end to doubt. The more one listens, the more one doubts. The more one listens, the more confused one becomes."

The Lord Buddha continued, "Doubt is not something that another person can resolve for us. Another person can only explain about doubt; it is for us to apply to our own experience and come to direct knowledge ourselves."

The Buddha taught, "Within this body are form, feelings, perceptions, thoughts, and consciousness. These are already our teachers, giving us knowledge; but it requires proper meditation and investigation. If you wish to make an end of doubt, then you should stop and investigate this body and mind.

"Discard the past. Whatever good one has done, whatever evil one has done, discard them. There is no benefit in holding on to them now. Whatever was good has passed. Whatever was wrong has passed.

"The future has not yet come. Whatever will be will arise and pass away in the future. When it does, you should recognize it and discard it without grasping.

"Whatever occurred in the past has vanished. Why will you expend yourself thinking about it now? In the present you need not be involved with it. You need not try to stop any thoughts or recognition, but having thought of and recognized the past, you are aware of this and let it go, because it is something that is already finished.

"The future has not yet come. Knowing thoughts of the future as they arise and pass away, let them go. Thoughts of the past are impermanent. The future is uncertain. Knowing them, let them go. Look at the present, right now. Look at the here and now Dharma of your present experience. Do not think that this or that teacher will resolve your doubts for you."

———

The Buddha did not praise those who believe others. One who relies on the words of others and is elated or depressed thereby is not praised by the Buddha. Understanding what someone says, one should let go, because those words are another's and should not be attached to. Even if they are correct, they are correct for that person. If we don't internalize them and make them correct in our own hearts, they never really become correct for us, and the doubts do not cease. "Is it correct? Is that teacher right? Is this teacher wrong?" This means that we haven't practiced to realize the true meaning, so we are not yet praised by the Buddha.

I am always teaching about this aspect of the Dharma that calls for turning inward to see, to know, and to realize for yourself. If someone says something is right, don't yet believe him. If he says something is wrong, don't yet believe him. "Right" and "wrong" are merely words spoken by some other person. Whatever teaching you hear, internalize it and practice to realize the truth of it, here and now.

The same practice will not be the same for different individuals, because of their differing degrees of wisdom. We go to see meditation teachers and try to understand their way. We look at their methods and their conduct, but this is looking at externals. What we can see of their practice is just the external aspect. If this is how we approach it, then our doubts will always remain. "Why does this teacher practice in this way? Why does that teacher use that method? Why does one teach a lot, while another teaches very little, and another doesn't teach at all?" This can really confuse you.

Finding the right way doesn't depend on these things. It's up to each individual to follow the correct path. We can take others as good examples, but we have to look deeper within ourselves in order to eradicate the doubts. Thus the Buddha taught that elder to contemplate the present moment, not letting his mind go off toward past or future.

So in all situations, he kept on watching the mind. Whatever conditions there were, it didn't matter—he saw that they are uncertain, that they are impermanent. Only this is what the Buddha taught him, and through practicing it he was able to realize the Dharma, to realize that the truth was within himself.

The wheel of *samsara,* the round of existence, spins, but it's not necessary to try to follow after it. It goes around in a circle—do you want to try to keep up with it? It's really fast. If a wheel is spinning, you can stay in one place and let it spin around. A lizard might try to run after it; you can stay put and see the lizard come around again and again without having to chase it. It's fast, the cycle of the worldly dharmas. But for a person who has wisdom, there is no problem. If one is mindful, then in all different situations, coming and going, taking care of whatever affairs one has to, there is no harm to the mind.

PART THREE

DUKKHA

Unsatisfactoriness

16

Understanding Dukkha

DUKKHA STICKS ON THE skin and goes into the flesh; from the flesh, it gets into the bones. It's like an insect on a tree that eats through the bark, into the wood, and then into the core, until finally the tree dies.

As we grow up, it gets buried deep inside. Our parents teach us grasping and attachment, giving meaning to things, believing firmly that we exist as a self-entity and that things belong to us. From our birth that's what we are taught. We hear this over and over again, and it penetrates our hearts and stays there as our habitual feeling. We're taught to get things, to accumulate and hold on to them, to see them as important and as ours. This is what our parents know, and this is what they teach us. So it gets into our minds, into our bones.

When we take an interest in meditation and hear the teaching of a spiritual guide, it's not easy to understand. It doesn't really grab us. We're taught not to see and do things the old way, but when we hear this, it doesn't penetrate our hearts.

So we sit and listen to teachings, but it's often just sound entering the ears. It doesn't get inside and affect us. It's like we're boxing, and we keep hitting the other guy but he doesn't go down. We remain stuck in our self-view. The wise have said that moving a mountain from one place to another is easier than moving the conceit of self-view, this solid feeling that we really exist as some special individual.

We can use explosives to level a mountain and then move the earth. But the tight grasping of self-conceit—oh man! Our wrong ideas and bad tendencies remain so solid and unbudging, and we're not aware of them. So the wise have said that removing this view and turning wrong understanding into right understanding is about the hardest thing to do.

For us who are worldly beings (*putthujana*) to progress on to being virtuous beings (*kalyanajana*) is not easy. A putthujana is one who is thickly obscured, who is dark, who is stuck deep in this darkness and obscuration. The kalyanajana has made things lighter. We teach people to lighten, but they don't want to do that, because they don't understand their situation, their condition of obscuration. So they keep on drifting in their confused state.

If we come across a pile of buffalo dung, we won't think it's ours and we won't want to pick it up. We will just leave it where it is, because we know what it is.

Such is what's good in the way of the impure. That which is evil is the food of bad people. If you teach them about doing good, they're not interested, but prefer to stay as they are because they don't see the harm in it. Without seeing the harm, there's no way things can be rectified. If you recognize it, then you think, "Oh! My whole pile of dung doesn't have the value of a small piece of gold!" and you will want gold instead; you won't want the dung anymore. If you don't recognize this, you remain the owner of a pile of dung.

That's the "good" of the impure. Gold, jewels, and diamonds are considered something good in the realm of humans. The foul and rotten are good for flies and other insects. If you gather fresh flowers, the flies won't be interested in them. Even if you tried to pay them, they wouldn't come. But wherever there's a dead animal, wherever there's something rotten, that's where they'll go. Wrong view is like that. It delights in that kind of thing. What's sweet-smelling to a bee is not sweet to a fly.

There were once two close friends. After they died, one was reborn among the gods of sensual enjoyment, while the other was born as a maggot in a pit of excrement.

The god was endowed with various powers, and recalling his dear friend from the past life, he used his clairvoyance to find him. He transported himself to the excrement pit and was able to get his friend to recognize him. They were joyful at meeting again.

The maggot asked the god, "So what's it like where you were reborn?"

The god said, "It's great! Nothing but pure enjoyment! Everything is clean and delightful. Whatever you wish for, it appears instantly. I hope you can go there with me."

But the maggot started crying, because he pitied his friend. "Listen," he said. "Life is so much fun right here. I play all day in this pit. I don't even have to wish for what I want to appear, because it's all right here. You really ought to stay."

There is difficulty in practice, but in anything we undertake, we have to pass through difficulty to reach ease. In Dharma practice, we begin with the truth of dukkha, the pervasive unsatisfactoriness of existence. But as soon as we experience this, we lose heart. We don't want to look at it. Dukkha is really the truth, but we want to get around it somehow. It's similar to the way we don't like to look at old people, but prefer to look at the young and attractive.

If we don't want to look at dukkha, we will never understand dukkha, no matter how long we live. Dukkha is truth. If we allow ourselves to face it, then we will start to seek a way out of it. If we're trying to go somewhere and the road is blocked, we will think about how to make a pathway. Working at it day after day, we can get through. When we encounter problems, we develop wisdom like this. Without seeing dukkha, we don't really look into and resolve our problems; we just bear with them or pass them by indifferently.

My way of training people involves some suffering, because understanding suffering is the Buddha's path to enlightenment. He wanted us to see suffering, and to see its origination, its cessation, and the path that brings about cessation. This is the way out for all the awakened ones. If you don't go this way, there is no way out.

If we know dukkha, we will see it in everything we experience. Some people feel that they don't really suffer much. But practice in Buddhism is for the purpose of freeing ourselves from suffering, the unsatisfactoriness that pervades ordinary experience. What should we do not to suffer anymore? When dukkha arises, we should investigate to see the causes of its arising. Knowing that, we can practice to remove those causes. Then once we travel the path to fulfillment, dukkha will no longer arise. In Buddhism, this is the way out.

Opposing our habits creates some suffering. But generally, we are afraid of suffering, and if something will make us suffer, we don't want to do it. We are interested in what appears to be good and beautiful, and we feel that anything involving suffering is bad. But it's not like that. If there is suffering in the heart, it becomes the cause that makes you think about escaping. It leads you to contemplate. You will be intent on investigating to find out what is really going on, trying to see causes and their results.

Happy people don't develop wisdom. They're asleep. It's like a dog that eats its fill. After that it doesn't want to do anything. It can sleep all day. It won't bark if a burglar comes—it's too full and too tired. But if you only give it a little food, it will be alert and awake. If someone comes sneaking around, it will jump up and start barking. Have you seen that?

We humans are trapped and imprisoned in this world and have troubles in such abundance, and we are always full of doubt, confusion, and worry. This is no game. So there's something we need to get rid of. According to the way of spiritual cultivation, we should give up our bodies, give up ourselves. We have to resolve to give our lives to the pursuit of liberation.

If we speak the subtle Dharma, most people will be frightened by it. They won't dare to enter it. Even saying, "Don't do evil," most people can't follow this. So I've sought all kinds of means to get this across, and one thing I often say is, no matter if we are delighted or upset, happy or suffering, shedding tears or singing songs, never mind—living in this world, we are living in a cage. We don't get beyond this condition of being in a cage. Even if you are rich, you are living in a cage. If you are poor, you are living in a cage. If you sing and dance, you're singing and dancing in a cage. If you watch a movie, you're watching it in a cage.

What is this cage? It's the cage of birth, the cage of aging, the cage of illness, the cage of death. In this way, we are imprisoned in the world. "This is mine." "That belongs to me." We don't know what we really are or what we're doing. Actually all we are doing is accumulating suffering for ourselves. It's not something far away that causes our suffering, but we don't look at ourselves. However much happiness and comfort we may have, having been born we cannot avoid aging, we must fall ill, and we must die. This is dukkha itself, here and now.

The time we can be afflicted with pain or illness is always. It can happen at any moment. It's like we've stolen something: we could be arrested at any time because we've done that. That's our situation. We exist among harmful things, among danger and trouble; aging, illness, and death reign over our lives. We can't go elsewhere and escape them. They can come catch us at any time—it's always a good opportunity for them. So we have to cede this to them and accept the situation. We have to plead guilty. If we do, the sentence won't be so heavy. If we don't, we suffer enormously.

If we plead guilty, they'll go easy on us—we won't be incarcerated too long.

When the body is born, it doesn't belong to anyone. It's like our meditation hall. After it's built, spiders come to stay in it. Lizards come to stay in it. All sorts of insects and crawling things come to stay in it. Snakes may come to live in it. Anything may come to live in it. It's not only our hall; it's everything's hall.

These bodies are the same. They aren't ours. We come to stay in and depend on them. Illness, pain, and aging come to reside in them, and we are merely residing along with them. When these bodies reach the end of pain and illness and finally break up and die, that is not us dying. So don't hold on to any of this, but contemplate clearly, and your grasping will gradually be exhausted.

Do you know if desire has limits? At what point will it be satisfied? Is there such a thing? If you consider it, you will see that *tanha,* blind craving, can't be satisfied. It keeps on desiring more and more; even if this brings such suffering that we are nearly dead, tanha will keep on wanting things, because satisfaction is not possible for it.

The Buddha taught the "Instructions for the Rich." It means being content with what we have. That is a rich person. This is the instruction for the rich.

I think this kind of knowledge is really worth studying. The knowledge taught in the Buddha's way is something worth learning, worth reflecting on. First, it teaches the way of ethical living. As long as we have enough material sustenance to support our lives, we can block the path to the lower realms by living morally.

Then, the pure Dharma of practice goes beyond that. It's a lot deeper. Some of us may not be able to understand it. Just take the Buddha's words that there is no more birth for him, that birth and becoming are finished. Hearing this makes us uncomfortable. To state it directly, the Buddha said that we should not be born, because that is suffering. Just this one thing, birth, the Buddha focused on, contemplating it and realizing its gravity. Being born, all dukkha comes along with that. It happens simultaneously with birth. When we come into this world, we get eyes, a mouth, a nose—it all comes along, only because of birth. But if we hear about dying and not being born again, we feel it would be utter ruination. We don't want to go there. But the deepest teaching of the Buddha is like this.

Why are we suffering now? Because we were born. So we are taught to put an end to birth. This is not just talking about the body being born and the body dying. That much is easy to see—a child can understand it. The breath comes to an end, the body dies, and then it just lies there. This is what we usually mean when we talk about death. But a breathing dead person—that's something we don't know about. A dead person who can walk and talk and smile is something we haven't thought about. We only know about the corpse that's no longer breathing. That's what we call death.

It's the same with birth. When we say someone has been born, we mean that a woman went to the hospital and gave birth. But the moment of the mind taking birth—have you noticed that, such as when you get upset over something at home? Sometimes love is born. Sometimes aversion is born. Being pleased, being displeased—all sorts of states. This is birth.

We suffer just because of this. When the eyes see something displeasing, dukkha is born. The ears hear something that you really like, and dukkha is also born. There is only suffering.

The Buddha summed it up by saying that there is only a mass of dukkha. Dukkha is born and dukkha ceases. That's all there is. We pounce on and grab at it again and again, pouncing on arising, pouncing on cessation, never really understanding it.

When dukkha arises, we call that suffering. When it ceases, we call that happiness. It's all old stuff, arising and ceasing. We are taught to watch body and mind arising and ceasing. There's nothing else outside of this.

We recognize suffering as suffering when it arises. Then when it ceases, we consider that to be happiness. We see it and designate it as such, but it isn't. It's just dukkha ceasing. Dukkha arises and ceases, arises and ceases, and we pounce on and grab hold of it. Happiness appears and we are pleased. Unhappiness appears and we are distraught. It's really all the same, mere arising and ceasing. When there is arising, there's something, and when there is ceasing, it's gone. This is where we become confused. Thus it's taught that dukkha arises and ceases, and outside of that, there is nothing.

We don't recognize clearly that there is only suffering because when it stops, we see happiness there. We seize on it and get stuck there. We don't really know what's going on, which is just arising and ceasing.

The Buddha summed things up by saying that there are only arising and ceasing, and there's nothing outside of that. This is difficult to listen to. But one who truly has a feel for the Dharma doesn't need to depend on anything and dwells in ease.

The truth is that in this world of ours, there is nothing that does anything to anybody. There is nothing to be anxious about. There's nothing worth crying over, nothing to laugh at. Nothing is inherently tragic or delightful. But such is what's ordinary for people.

Our speech can be ordinary, relating to others according to the ordinary way of seeing things. That's OK. But if we are thinking in the ordinary way, that leads to tears.

If we really know the Dharma and see it continuously, nothing is anything at all; there are only arising and passing away. There's no real happiness or suffering. The heart is at peace then, when there is no happiness or suffering. When there is happiness and suffering, there is becoming and birth, meaning ceaseless transformation.

We are usually trying to stop suffering to give rise to happiness. That's what we want. But what we want is not real peace; it's happiness and suffering. The aim of the Buddha's teaching is to practice to create a type of karma that is beyond happiness and suffering and that will bring peace. But usually, we can only think that having happiness will bring us peace. If we find some happiness, we think that's good enough.

Thus we humans wish for things in abundance. If we get a lot, that's good—generally, that's how we think. Doing good is supposed to bring good results, and if we get that, we're happy. We think that's all we need to do, and we stop there. But can good experiences give us lasting satisfaction? It doesn't remain. We keep going back and forth, experiencing good and bad, trying day and night to seize on what we feel is good.

The Buddha's teaching is that first we should give up evil, and then we practice what is good. Second, he said that we should give up evil and give up the good as well, not having attachment to it, because that is also one kind of fuel. When there is something that is fuel, it will eventually burst into flame. Good is fuel. Bad is fuel.

17

Shaking Up the Students

Ajahn Chah's Methods

AJAHN CHAH IS REMEMBERED as a fierce taskmaster by many, especially his older disciples. One, Ajahn Sinuan, related a story about a time they were working on one of the kutis. He was holding up a board for another monk to nail, and Ajahn Chah started discussing something with that monk, leaving Sinuan holding up the plank as wasps buzzed around him. Finally, arms aching unbearably, he said, "Luang Por ('Revered Father'), I don't think I can hold it much longer," upon which Ajahn Chah whacked him on the back with a stick. This left Sinuan shattered and convinced that Ajahn Chah was certainly inhumane.

That night, after the chanting service and meditation, Ajahn Chah gave a talk to the community. "I want all of you to think about why you are here. You should understand that everything I do is for the purpose of freeing you from the snares of Mara, nothing else. You have been prisoner to your habits your whole lives. If you didn't want to get free, why would you have come here?"

18

Birth and Becoming

IT'S TAUGHT THAT BIRTH is suffering, but it doesn't only mean dying from this life and taking rebirth in the next life. That's too far away. The suffering of birth happens right now. It's said that becoming is the cause of birth. What is this "becoming"? Anything that we attach to and put meaning on is becoming. Whenever we see anything as self or other or belonging to ourselves, without wise discernment to know that such is only a convention, that is becoming. Whenever we hold on to something as us or ours and it then undergoes change, the mind is shaken by that. It is shaken with a positive or negative reaction. That sense of self experiencing happiness or unhappiness is birth. When there is birth, it brings suffering along with it, because everything must change and disappear.

Right now, do we have becoming? Are we aware of this becoming? For example, take the trees in an orchard. The owner of the orchard can take birth as a worm in every single tree if he isn't aware of himself, if he feels that it's really his orchard. This grasping at "my" orchard and "my" trees is the worm that latches on there.

If there are thousands of trees, he will become a worm thousands of times. This is becoming. When the trees are cut or meet with any harm, the worms are affected; the mind is shaken and takes birth with all this anxiety. Then there is the suffering of birth, the suffering of aging, and so forth. Are you aware of the way this happens?

Well, those objects in our homes or our orchards are still a little far away. Let's look right at ourselves sitting here. We are composed of the five aggregates and the four elements. These *sankhara* are designated as a self. Do you see these sankhara and these designations as they really are? If you don't see the truth of them, there is becoming, being gladdened or depressed over the five khandhas, and you take birth, with all the resultant sufferings. This rebirth happens right now, in the present. This glass breaks right now, and we are upset right now. This glass isn't broken now, and we are happy about it now. This is how it happens, blindly being upset or being happy. One only meets with ruination. You don't need to look far away to understand this. When you pay attention to yourself, you can know whether or not there is becoming. It's the grasping attachment that is the vital point, whether or not we really believe in the designations of me and mine. This grasping is the worm, and it is what causes birth.

Grasping onto form, feeling, perception, thoughts, and consciousness, we attach to happiness and unhappiness, and we become obscured and take birth. It happens when we have contact through the senses. The eyes see forms and it happens in the present. This is what the Buddha wanted us to look at, to recognize becoming and birth as they occur through our senses. If we know them, we can let go, let go of the inner senses and their external objects. This can be seen in the present. It's not something that happens when we die from this life. It's the eye seeing forms right now, the ear hearing sounds right now, the nose smelling aromas right now, the tongue tasting flavors right now. Do you take birth with them? Be aware and recognize birth right as it happens.

~◇~

The previous *Sangharaja,* the Supreme Patriarch of the monastic order, once went on a tour of China, where someone offered him a very beautiful teacup. It was unlike anything he'd ever seen. He thought, "Oh! The people here have real faith in me, to offer me this beautiful teacup!" And as soon as the teacup was in his hand, immediately he was suffering. Where should I put it? Where is safe to keep it? He couldn't stop worrying it would break.

Before he had that teacup, he was fine. Once he had it, he wanted to show it off to the people back home in Thailand. He put it in his bag and kept telling everyone to watch out that the teacup didn't get broken. "Hey! Careful, please!" Everywhere he was watching out for it. He had nothing but suffering. Before, this suffering didn't exist, but now there was the heaviness of having the teacup.

So he boarded his plane back to Thailand. When he arrived he warned the novices, "Be careful! Don't let the teacup break! You laypeople, watch out! There's something fragile here!" This went on all the time, suffering because of attachment to the cup.

Finally, one day, a long time later, a novice picked it up and it slipped from his hand and broke. What relief the Sangharaja felt. "Ah, I am free! Suffering all these years."

19

Evanescence

Impermanent are all conditioned things,
Of the nature to arise and pass away.
Appearing, they disappear.
Their cessation is supreme bliss.
—*Pali funeral chant*

THE BUDDHA TAUGHT US to understand death, that this is the way things are; life is uncertain, and realizing this leads to disenchantment with the world. When we go from this world, whoever has a lot will be leaving a lot behind. Whoever has little will be leaving little behind. Nobody gets to keep anything. If you have a lot of land and money, you may think, "I will leave my vast estate to my children." But your children don't get to keep it either; they will also have to leave it behind someday. All things exist within these limits in this realm of uncertainty. Such is the world.

In our culture, people believe that a death is the time to accumulate a lot of merit. But it's more important to accumulate merit in the way you live. Coming to some real understanding and changing your ways in order to live virtuously will be genuine merit, something of definite value.

If you think clearly about life and death, you will realize that it's like mangoes growing on a tree. They grow to maturity, and then they fall and hit the ground. When that has happened, the mangoes won't be longing for the tree, and the tree won't be worried about the mangoes.

Our lives are like this. When we understand this, we won't be heedless. We will turn our attention to thinking about how we should live and spend our time and what we will practice.

We want to be free of suffering. We want to remove suffering from our hearts, but still we suffer. Why is this? It's because of wrong thinking. If our thinking is in harmony with the way things are, we will have well-being. Practicing Dharma means seeking right understanding. For example, look at our bodies. Are they really ours? They are born, they change, and they die of their own. We can't stop them from doing that; we can't order them to be a certain way. So we keep investigating and looking at the facts, asking ourselves if this is really the case, and we see that we do not have the power to control these impermanent bodies according to our wishes. When we see this, the mind changes and enters the Dharma. Looking continuously at the nature of sankhara, we come to see that our bodies are unreliable, and we are led to see the noble truth of suffering.

But we are so fearful. When we're told to think about death, we are afraid to do it. When we hear the teachings on impermanence, suffering, and not-self, we don't want to listen. The Buddha said this is something we should take interest in and contemplate. But people are so afraid. They only want birth, without death. They only want to have good things. That's pretty silly. Can you get this? Think deeply for a moment.

The teachings say, "Impermanent are all conditioned things, of the nature to arise and pass away." Well, what is this impermanence all about? These "conditioned things" are just what is sitting here right at this moment. We will all meet this fate, without exception. But we don't face up to it and investigate.

There's nothing better than investigating this. These days the doctors are investigating cancer, but they can't seem to find a cure for it. Why aren't they trying to cure the disease of death instead? The disease of death is much more fearsome than cancer. When I went abroad, I was having it out with a bunch of doctors over this: the disease of death is something really worth taking an interest in. Why haven't you been researching it? If we do contemplate it, then our wrong actions will start decreasing. People are concerned with cancer. But the disease of aging is worse than cancer. The disease of death is contracted by every living being. Those with cancer will die. Those without cancer will die. So the disease of death is what's really important to analyze.

When we teach people to practice recollection of death, they say, "Don't talk about it! If you talk about death, no one will want to do anything!" Such thinking is really mistaken. This disease is the chronic disease of life. The Buddha wanted us to look and realize that all beings without exception are in this condition. It's the truth, so he taught us not to forget or have illusions about it. If you do recollect death regularly, you will cease to harm others. You will see there's no point in doing evil and taking it with you when you die. This is something that can have benefit to yourself, to your family, and to society.

Someone who has done a lot of bad things will start making efforts to give up old ways. Bad actions not yet done we will avoid in future. Defilements of mind will gradually keep decreasing. Then when we attempt to instruct others, we will be setting a good example for them, and we will really be able to help them.

Think about a person who is condemned to death: In fifteen days, say, or in a month, she is going to face a firing squad. How would we use our time if this fate were ours? What would we think? Consider it for a moment—what would go through your mind? You could probably eat salt and not taste the saltiness.

One day we are going to die. The time is not set. It could be in a day or two. It could be after a long time. So we all have to think very clearly that we are like someone sentenced to death— like a criminal languishing in jail, just waiting to be taken, or like cows in the slaughterhouse, with red marks on their sides: today this one gets slaughtered, tomorrow that one, the day after, that one. We are just like that herd of cows. So would you be joking around in there, singing songs and amusing yourself?

This is really the situation we're in. So the Buddha taught us to build those things that are of benefit. We don't build them with material wealth, but with efforts of body and speech and with the energy of wise discernment. Each day we should do at least one meritorious act. At the very least you can show kindness to an animal. Don't let a day go by without creating virtue.

The life of all beings is uncertain. When we understand this, then we can be more relaxed about what we do in this world. We won't take the ups and downs of events too seriously, and we won't have upset, disappointment, or fear. We won't be taking extreme delight in things either; whether we live or die, we have built our safe haven with good deeds.

There's no other time to practice. You have to do it while you're still living. When you are taught about doing good and creating virtue, work at that now and you will get the results. After you die it's too late; there's only the funeral. When you die they come to pay respects; you are then just an object they can practice merit on. The merit you had is all finished. But if you keep creating it now, while you are alive, it doesn't get exhausted so fast.

20

Cold Comfort

Ajahn Chah's Monks Face Illness and Death

THE FACT OF OUR mortality displays very obviously the three characteristics—impermanence, unsatisfactoriness, and lack of self. But this contemplation is no study in morbidity. Honest awareness of death can lead to the deathless, just as honest awareness of suffering can lead us beyond suffering, and recognizing what binds us to the mundane can lead to freedom.

Generally, death is more accepted in Buddhist cultures such as Thailand than it is in the West, and in the monastic environment in particular there is no tiptoeing around it. Ajahn Chah talked about death in different ways to different people, just as he did with other aspects of the Dharma. When people are a little more high-minded, he said, you can poke them to wake them up. In the early years of Wat Pah Pong, one of the many hardships the monks faced was malaria. There was no treatment available, and most of them became severely ill. He told of how he encouraged the monks to face the situation.

"One night, about nine o'clock, I heard someone walking out of the forest. We were all sick with malaria, but one monk was in a really bad way, with high fever, and was afraid he would die. He didn't want to die alone in the forest. I said, 'That's good. Let's try to find someone who isn't ill to watch the one who is; how can one sick person take care of another?' That was about it. We didn't have any medicine.

"We had *borapet* (a horribly bitter medicinal vine). We boiled it to drink. It was all we had, for refreshment or for medicine. Everyone had fever and everyone drank borapet. If any monks got really sick, I told them, 'Don't be afraid. Don't worry. If you die, I'll cremate you myself. I'll cremate you right here in the monastery. Your corpse won't have to go anywhere else.' This is how I dealt with it. These words gave them strength of mind."

21

The Buddha Didn't Die

LET'S PLEASE MEDITATE ON this subject of our mortality properly, meditate and look into this until we can think more deeply—such as, how is our existence going to change from this moment on? What can we do about it?

Fools cry over death. They don't cry over birth. But where does death come from? Doesn't it come from birth? If you cry about people dying, you should cry when people are born. As soon as someone is born, start crying immediately: "Oh no, she's come again! She's going to die again!" Talk like that—it's more correct that way.

But now we try to use things like magic, prayers, and incantations to ward off death. What's the point of that? Why don't we try to solve the problem at the source, which is birth? This is like a boxer who gets his teeth knocked out and then ducks. You have to duck before they slug you. These things are useless; the Buddha taught about it.

The Buddha taught that, having been born, we should find a path to escape from death. The Buddha did not die! The *arahants* (those who have attained liberation) do not die! They don't die as people and animals do. When death comes to them, they will be all smiles. They will be at ease, because they don't die. This is something people can't understand. They can't see it. The Buddha didn't die. The arahants don't die. Earth, water, fire, air, the four elements, simply split up; there is no person in these things. So we say the enlightened ones don't die. They are not born, they do not age, they don't fall ill, they don't die. Craving, anger, and delusion are not born in them anymore. While they are still living, their bodies are not theirs or themselves. There are heaps of earth, water, fire, and air, and then those things simply break up and disperse. They don't hold to there being any person in them. Those things don't affect them, so we say they don't die. But we depend on these heaps. We call them a person. We believe them to be ourselves and others, and when they break up we think that we die, and so we suffer. The enlightened ones do not suffer over this. Dirt, they call it. A pile of dirt! By seeing that there are only earth, water, fire, and air, they conquer death.

22

Birth, Death, and Enlightenment

Ajahn Chah and the Bodhi Tree

ON THE OCCASION OF Visakha Puja, the Buddhist holiday commemorating the birth, enlightenment, and death of the Buddha, Ajahn Chah said, "When the Buddha attained enlightenment, we can say that he died to the worldly way and was born as the Buddha. Visakha Puja really means this one fact of his enlightenment; there weren't three separate events that we commemorate."

⌒

Someone told Ajahn Chah about a friend who went to practice with a Zen teacher and asked, "When the Buddha sat beneath the bodhi tree, what was he doing?" The Zen master answered, "He was practicing zazen!" But the man said, "I don't believe it."

The Zen master asked him, "What do you mean, you don't believe it?" and the man replied, "I asked Goenka-ji (a renowned vipassana teacher) the same question, and he said, 'When the Buddha was sitting under the bodhi tree, he was practicing vipassana!' So everybody says the Buddha was doing whatever they do."

Ajahn Chah remarked, "When the Buddha sat out in the open, he was sitting beneath the bodhi tree. When he sat under some other kind of tree, he was sitting beneath the bodhi tree. There's nothing wrong with those explanations. 'Bodhi' means the Buddha himself, the one who knows. It's OK to talk about sitting beneath the bodhi tree, but lots of birds sit beneath the bodhi tree. Lots of people sit beneath the bodhi tree. Monkeys play in the bodhi tree. But this doesn't mean they have any profound understanding. Those who have deeper understanding realize that the true meaning of 'the bodhi tree' is the absolute Dharma.

"So in this way, it's certainly good for us to try to sit beneath the bodhi tree. Then we can be Buddha. But we don't need to argue with others over this question. When one person says the Buddha was doing one kind of practice beneath the bodhi tree and another person disputes that, we needn't get involved. We should be looking at it from the viewpoint of the ultimate, meaning realizing the truth. There's also the conventional idea of 'bodhi tree,' which is what most people talk about, but if people end up arguing and having contentious disputes, then there is no bodhi tree at all."

PART FOUR

ANATTA

Not-Self

23

Practice Like the Four Elements

A CITY PERSON MAY like to eat mushrooms. He asks, "Where do the mushrooms come from?" and someone tells him, "They grow in the earth." So he picks up a basket and goes walking out into the countryside, expecting the mushrooms will be lined up along the side of the road for him to pick. But he walks and walks, climbing hills and trekking through fields, without seeing any mushrooms. A villager has gone picking mushrooms before, and she knows where to look for them; she knows which part of which forest to go to. But the city person only has the experience of seeing mushrooms on his plate. He heard they grow in the earth and got the idea that they would be easy to find, but it didn't work out that way.

Training the mind in *samadhi,* meditative stability, is similar. We get the idea it will be easy. But when we sit, our legs hurt, our back hurts, we feel tired, we get hot and itchy. Then we start to feel discouraged, thinking that samadhi is as far away from us as the sky from the earth. We don't know what to do and become overwhelmed by the difficulties. But if we can receive some training, it will get easier little by little.

When we are new to it, training in samadhi is difficult. Anything is difficult when we don't know how to do it. But training at it, this can change. That which is useful can eventually overcome and surpass that which is not. We tend to become fainthearted as we struggle—this is a normal reaction, and we all go through it. So it's important to train for some time. It's like making a path through the forest. At first it's rough going, with a lot of obstructions, but returning to it again and again, we clear the way. After a while, we have removed the branches and stumps, and the ground becomes firm and smooth from being walked on repeatedly. Then we have a good path for walking through the forest. This is what it's like when we train the mind. Keeping at it, the mind becomes illumined. The Buddha and his disciples were once ordinary beings, but they developed themselves to progress through the stages of enlightenment. They did this through training.

What was the Buddha's advice on how to practice meditation? He taught to practice like the earth, to practice like water, to practice like fire, to practice like wind. Practice like the "old things," the things we are already made of: the solid element of earth, the liquid element of water, the warming element of fire, the moving element of wind.

If someone digs the earth, the earth is not bothered. It can be shoveled, tilled, or watered. Rotten things can be buried in it. But the earth will remain indifferent. Water can be boiled or frozen or used to wash something dirty; it is not affected. Fire can burn beautiful and fragrant things or ugly and foul things—it doesn't matter to the fire. When wind blows, it blows on all sorts of things, fresh and rotten, without concern.

The Buddha used this analogy. The aggregation that is us is merely a coming together of the elements of earth, water, fire, and air. If you try to find an actual person there, you can't. There are only these collections of elements. But for all our lives, we never thought to separate them like this to see what's really there; we have only thought, "This is me. This is mine." We've always seen everything in terms of a self, never seeing that there are merely earth, water, fire, and air. But the Buddha teaches in this way. He talks about the four elements and urges us to see that this is what we are. There are earth, water, fire, and air; there is no person here. Contemplate these elements to see that there is no being or individual, but only earth, water, fire, and air.

It's deep, isn't it? It's hidden deep—people will look but they can't see it. We're used to thinking in terms of self and other all the time. So our meditation is still not very deep. It doesn't reach the truth, and we don't get beyond the way things appear to be. We remain stuck in the conventions of the world, and being stuck in the world means remaining in the cycle of transformation: getting things and losing them, dying and being born, being born and dying, suffering in the realm of confusion. Whatever we wish for and aspire to doesn't really work out the way we want, because we are seeing things wrongly. With this kind of grasping attachment, we are still very far indeed from the real path of Dharma.

Let's get to work right now. Our practice of Dharma should be getting us beyond suffering. If we can't fully transcend suffering, then we should at least be able to transcend it a little, now, in the present. For example, when someone speaks harshly to us, if we don't get angry, we have transcended suffering. If we get angry, we haven't transcended dukkha.

When someone speaks harshly to us, if we reflect on Dharma, we will see it is just heaps of earth involved. OK, he is criticizing me—he's just criticizing a heap of earth. One heap of earth is criticizing another heap of earth. Water is criticizing water. Air is criticizing air. Fire is criticizing fire.

But if we really see things in this way, then others will probably call us mad. "He doesn't care about anything. He has no feelings!" When someone dies we won't get upset and cry, and they will call us crazy.

It really comes down to practicing and realizing for ourselves. Getting beyond suffering doesn't depend on others' opinions of us, but on our own individual state of mind. Never mind what they will say—if we experience the truth for ourselves, then we can dwell at ease.

When difficulties occur, recollect Dharma. Think of what your spiritual guides have taught you. They teach you to let go, to have restraint and self-control, to put things down; they teach you to strive in this way to solve your problems. The Dharma that you study is just for solving your problems.

What kind of problems are we talking about? How about your families? Do you have any problems there? Any problems with your children, your spouses, your friends, or your work? All these things give you headaches sometimes, don't they? These are the problems we are talking about; the teachings are telling you that you can resolve the problems of daily life with Dharma.

We have been born as human beings. It should be possible to live with happy minds. We do our work according to our responsibilities. If things get difficult, we practice endurance. Earning a livelihood in the right way is one sort of Dharma practice, the practice of ethical living. Living happily and harmoniously like this is already pretty good.

We are usually taking a loss, however. Don't take a loss! If you go to a center or a monastery to meditate and then go home and fight, that's a loss. Do you hear what I'm saying? It's just a loss to do this. It means you don't see the Dharma even a tiny little bit—there's no profit at all.

24

Ignorance

Ajahn Chah Holds Up a Mirror

A FORMER NUN TOLD this story of her first meeting with Ajahn Chah. Having heard much about him, she went to see him at the Hampstead Vihara when he was in London in 1979. He asked her if she practiced meditation, and when she said she had attended several retreats, he asked about her understanding of anatta.

"I began to talk, and I got into this long, complicated explanation. I was going on and on talking about not-self, and as I spoke, I felt my sense of self expanding like a balloon," she said.

When she finished talking, Ajahn Chah said a few words in Thai.

"What did he say?" she asked.

"He says you're very ignorant," the translator supplied.

Yet rather than feeling denigrated, the young woman was attracted by Ajahn Chah's obvious loving kindness as he spoke those words, and she eventually traveled to Thailand to take ordination with him.

25

Not Us, Not Ours

TRADITIONALLY, THE LUNAR QUARTER days are considered by Buddhists to be observance days, or "monastic days," in which laypeople can spend the day in a monastery for teaching and practice. This is an ancient Buddhist custom. Our forebears divided the month into twenty-six days for lay life and four days for monastic practice. The lay life gets a lot more days.

Having some chance to train in Dharma is important for us. The Buddha said, "Days and nights are relentlessly passing; how are we using the time?" He was afraid we would become forgetful and heedless, so he reminded us about the days passing. And it's not simply days passing—our lives are passing. We are constantly aging, constantly getting older, and then one day it will be finished. So the Buddha posed this question, "Days and nights are relentlessly passing; how well are we using our time?"

The Buddha exhorted us again and again to contemplate in the present: Where have we come from? Why have we come? Who is it that brought us here and is leading us on? Do we know how many years or months we will stay? When we leave here, where are we headed?

When we recollect the passing of days and nights, we will constantly be contemplating these questions. When we do think about them constantly, we will come to realize that human life is not long. From children we become adults, and then suddenly we are old. The transformation is happening every day. If we look at this, we will pay serious attention to our lives and our actions.

Thus, our ancestors made the custom of setting aside the four days a month as monastic days. Twenty-six days are layfolks' days, for doing worldly work and earning a living; having taken care of business, then you have the other four days to go to a monastery or Dharma center and take a break. There you can hear teachings and get some different ideas. When you are at home, all you are hearing and thinking is, "This is us. That is ours." Everything is "us" and "ours." You never hear anyone saying, "Nothing is ours." But when you come to the monastery and listen to a sermon, the ajahn will say, "This is not us; those things are not ours."

"Hey, what's that about?" you will wonder. "Why do they talk like that? All these things are certainly mine. I've worked so hard over the years to gather them. Is the teacher lying? Why does he say, 'This is not us. That is not ours'?" You don't know what to make of it at first. You don't know what to believe. You've always had the idea in your mind that "this is me; these things are mine."

But whenever you come to the monastery, you keep hearing the same thing: "This is not us. That is not ours." The conflict goes on. The world and the Dharma are in conflict. The world will not give up its viewpoint: This is us. These things are ours. But the ajahns keep telling you, "This is not us. These things are not ours."

After some time, after getting these reminders regularly and looking at your experience, you can start to gain insight into the way things really are, and your thinking will change. Then you will recognize that what the ajahns have been telling you is true. But if you only come once in a while, then you are hearing one thing in the monastery, and as soon as you go back home you will be hearing and thinking something else, and the struggle and dissonance go on. It will take a long time of going back and forth to see the truth and make up your mind. You have to go through this, experiencing confusion as to who is telling the truth. But thinking it through and meditating on it, you can start to see clearly.

Listening to Dharma has value like this. Over time it sinks in, and you begin to investigate sincerely and persistently. Learning about the shortcomings of the world, becoming aware of your aging, you begin to take it to heart. Most people resist hearing these things at first, but after some time we may come around. Then we realize that the teachings are true: What is called "ours" is just a convention. What we call "me" is just a convention.

Consider the things you have at home. Does anything ever break or get lost? Do things change? This is an example to help you see. If they are yours, why don't they obey what you tell them? And never mind these external possessions—how about your own body? Why do you get sick? If you are really the owner of your body, why would you let it get sick? The body is only earth, water, fire, and air. But having been born into these bodies, we believe they are really ours, so we are always struggling with them, with these impermanent phenomena. But there's no way we can win. We are always meeting with defeat, and in the end we separate from them. We can't negotiate the time of our death. We can't say, "Let my children grow up first. Let me make some money first." You can't do that. When the time comes, that's it. "But what will become of my family? Who will support my spouse and children? Who will take care of my parents?" It's no use. Death doesn't ask you about these matters first.

If we think about this, we will approach and enter the Dharma genuinely. It's like seeing a poisonous snake, such as a cobra, that comes slithering along. It has a lot of poison, and if we don't know what it is or we don't see it, we won't be cautious of it and we might step on it and be bitten.

We know what a cobra is. We know it is poisonous. When we see one coming, we recognize it and don't go close to it. We keep a safe distance, and then we won't be harmed. Even though the snake is poisonous, we aren't affected. We leave it alone and protect ourselves. The poison is still there, but it's as if it weren't, and we don't have to suffer.

Like this, we recognize what is harmful, and we stay away from it. Body and mind are their own sort of poisonous snakes. Have you ever noticed this? When your body is healthy and strong, you are exuberant: "Oh yes, the stars are in my favor!" But sometimes you are tormented by illness or pain and you moan, "Oh man, what kind of karma is this?" That's a poisonous snake.

It's the same for the mind. If things are going well, you are pleased and feel that life is not bad. Then something upsets you, and you may lose sleep over it, lying in bed with your tears flowing. It's poisonous like this. The snake is biting us, but we aren't aware of it.

The Buddha wanted us to study Dharma to know our own minds and bodies. Every morning in the monastery chanting service, we recite, "Bodily form is impermanent. Sensation is impermanent. Perception is impermanent. Thinking is impermanent. Consciousness is impermanent." And then, "Bodily form is not oneself or one's own," and so on for the other aggregates. Throughout mind and body, there is nothing but impermanence. There is nothing that is us or ours. Existing and then gone, appearing and passing away. This is the way it is, at all times and in all places.

Some people will hear the words, "Nothing is mine," and they will get the idea they should throw away all their possessions. With only superficial understanding, people will get into arguments about what this means and how to apply it. But this is something to contemplate carefully. "This is not my self" doesn't mean you should end your life or throw away your possessions. It means you should give up attachment.

There is the level of conventional reality and the level of ultimate reality—supposition and liberation. On the level of convention, there is Mr. A, Mrs. B, Mr. M., Mrs. N., and so on. We use these suppositions for convenience in communicating and functioning in the world. The Buddha did not teach that we shouldn't use these things, but that we shouldn't be attached to them as something ultimately real. We should realize that they are empty.

If we only look superficially, things appear to be real. But if we investigate thoroughly, to the core, they are merely so much: merely body, merely mind, merely happiness, merely suffering. That's all. In the end, if we don't understand these things, they are poisonous, like the cobra that can kill us and that we pick up or step on because we don't know what it is.

If the mind isn't aware of its desires and defilements, we suffer. They can lead us into a lot of confusion and conflict. When the body undergoes its natural course of change, we cry and lament over it. These are the poisonous snakes of body and mind.

The terrible sufferings that people experience are only products of their own minds. Some people are very fearful. It's because they let their minds run wild, thinking things over excessively. When they are alone in some dark place, they become terrified, thinking of ghosts or whatever, and they may jump up and run away. It's only thinking that makes them run. The ignorant mind proliferates its thoughts in this way. It is not us, not ours, not certain in the slightest way—but it can be trained. If one is bold, one will think differently, increasing boldness and driving out feelings of fear.

So we have twenty-six laypeople's days, and four monastic days to come and train. If we can't go to a monastery or a center, we should understand what their purpose is, and train ourselves in the practice at home. It's good not to forget the principle of observance days. You have a lot of days to take care of your affairs, so on occasion you can stop working to earn a living and instead spend time training your hearts. Having had some teaching and training, you can then return to your livelihood. The heart will become disturbed and confused, so you return to train again. And then you go back to your work. You learn to make your way in the world like this, learning the correct path so that you can earn your living without suffering over it. You come to understand impermanence. You see that being attached to impermanent and uncertain phenomena will always bring unsatisfactory results.

So this is the division handed down by the wise, to set aside four days of the month for spiritual training. It's a time for contemplation, to hear teachings, and to think and meditate on them. If all thirty days are for worldly living, it will probably lead to more difficulty. Twenty-six is enough.

26

Don't Be a Buddha

No matter what kind of Dharma we learn, if we don't realize the ultimate truth in our hearts, we won't reach satisfaction.

An apple is something you can see with your eyes. You can't know the flavor of the apple by looking at it. But you do see the apple. You can't see the flavor, but it's there. You can only know it when you pick up the apple and eat it.

The Dharma we teach is like the apple. Merely hearing it, people don't really know the flavor; when they practice, then it can be known. The flavor of the apple can't be known by the eyes, and the truth of the Dharma can't be known by the ears. There is knowledge, true, but it doesn't reach the actuality. One has to put it into practice. Then wisdom arises and one recognizes the ultimate truth directly. One sees the Buddha there. So I compare it to an apple in this way.

In order to help his disciples realize the Dharma, the Buddha taught a single path, but with different approaches and characteristics. He didn't use only one form of teaching or present the Dharma in the same way for everyone. But he taught for the single purpose of realizing ultimate truth and transcending suffering; all the meditations he taught were for this one purpose.

Questions and Answers

Student: Some people believe that Buddhism is nihilistic and wants to destroy the world.

Ajahn Chah: Their understanding is not complete or mature. They are afraid everything will be finished, that the world will come to an end. They conceive of Dharma as something empty and nihilistic, so they are disheartened when they hear it. But their way only leads to tears.

Have you seen what it's like when people are afraid of "emptiness"? Householders try to gather possessions and watch over them, like rats. Does this protect them from the emptiness of existence? They still end up on the funeral pyre, everything lost to them. But while they are alive they are trying to hold on to things, every day afraid they will be lost, trying to avoid emptiness. Do they suffer this way? Of course, they really do suffer. It's because of not understanding the real insubstantiality and emptiness of things; not understanding this, people are not happy.

Because people don't look at themselves, they don't really know what's going on in life. How do you stop this delusion? People believe, "This is me. This is mine." If you tell them about not-self, that nothing is me or mine, they immediately want to argue the point.

Even the Buddha, after he attained awakening, felt weary at heart when he considered this. When he was first enlightened, he thought it would be too hard to explain the way to others. But then he realized that such an attitude was mistaken.

If we don't teach such people, who will we teach? This is my question, which I used to ask myself at those times I got fed up and didn't want to teach anymore: who should we teach, if we don't teach the deluded? There's really nowhere else to go. When we get fed up and want to run away from others, we are deluded.

Student: How about if we aspire to be *pacceka buddhas* (the "solitary realizers" who attain enlightenment without a teacher and don't teach others)?

Ajahn Chah: Such terms are merely metaphors for states of mind. But being something is a burden. Don't be anything! Don't be anything at all! Being a buddha is a burden. Being a pacceka is a burden. Just don't desire to be. "I am Mr. Smith." "I am a venerable monk." That way is suffering, believing that you really exist thus. "Mr. Smith" is merely a convention. "Monk" is merely a convention.

If you believe you really exist, that brings suffering. If there is Mr. Smith, then when someone criticizes him, Mr. Smith gets angry. That's what happens if we hold these things to be real. Mr. Smith gets involved and is ready to fight. If there's no Mr. Smith, then there's no one there—no one to answer the telephone. *Ring ring*—nobody picks it up. You don't become anything. No one is being anything, and there is no suffering.

Once a monk came to see me, and he urgently confided, "Luang Por, I have attained stream entry (the first level of enlightenment)!"

All I could think to say was, "Well, that's a little better than being a dog, I guess." (Calling someone a dog is among the worst of insults in Thailand, and not done lightly by anyone.) He didn't like that, and he went away in a great huff. The stream enterer was angry!

If we believe ourselves to be something or someone, then every time the phone rings, we pick it up and get involved. How can we free ourselves of this? We have to look at it clearly and develop wisdom, so that there is no Mr. Smith to pick up the telephone. If you are Mr. Smith and you answer the telephone, you will get yourself involved in suffering. So don't be Mr. Smith. Just recognize that these names and titles are on the level of convention.

If someone calls you good, don't be that. Don't think, "I am good." If someone says you are bad, don't think, "I'm bad." Don't try to be anything. Know what is taking place. But then don't attach to the knowledge either, thinking, "I am someone who is aware."

People can't do this. They don't know what it's all about. I like to use the analogy of upstairs and downstairs. When you go down from upstairs, you are downstairs, and you see the downstairs. When you go upstairs again, you see the upstairs. The space in between you don't see. It means nirvana is not seen.

We see the physical form of things, but we don't see the grasping, the grasping at upstairs and downstairs. That is becoming and birth. We live continually becoming something. The place without becoming is empty. When we try to teach people about the place that is empty, they just say, "There's nothing there." Real practice is required for it to be known.

We have been relying on becoming, on self-grasping, since the day of our birth. When someone talks about not-self, it's too strange; we can't change our perceptions so easily. So it's necessary to make the mind see this through practice, and then we can believe it: "Oh! It's really true!"

When people are thinking, "This is mine! This is mine!" they feel happy. But when the thing that is "mine" is lost, then they will cry over it. This is the path for suffering to come about. We can observe this. If there is no "mine" or "me," then we can make use of things while we are living, without attachment to them as being ours. If they are lost or broken, that is simply natural; we don't see them as ours, or as anyone's, and we don't conceive of self or other.

I think what it comes down to is that people are afraid of change and afraid of death. Having been born, they don't want to die. But is that logical? It's like pouring water into a glass but not wanting it to fill up. If you keep pouring the water, you can't expect it not to be full. But people are born and don't want to die. Think about it. If people are born but never die, will that bring happiness? If no one who comes into the world dies, things will be a lot worse. We would probably all end up eating excrement! Where would we all stay? It's like pouring water into the glass without ceasing yet still not wanting it to be full. We really ought to think things through. If we really don't want to die, we should realize the deathless, as the Buddha taught. Do you know what the deathless means?

Though you die, if you have the wisdom of realizing anatta, it's as if you don't die. Not dying, not being born—that's where things can be finished. Being born and wishing for happiness and enjoyment without dying are not at all the correct way. But that's what people want, so there is no end of suffering for them. True practitioners do not suffer. Ordinary practitioners still suffer, because they haven't yet fulfilled the path of practice. They haven't realized the deathless, so they still suffer. They are still subject to death.

Born of the womb, can we avoid death? Apart from realizing that there is no real self, there is no way to avoid death. "I" don't die; *sankhara* (conditioned phenomena) undergo transformation, following their nature.

When others look at such a person and try to figure him out, they will probably see someone who's crazy. But this isn't a mad person; this is someone who is diligent. Such a person really knows what is useful, in so many different ways.

When an awakened being looks at ordinary, worldly people, she will see them as ignorant, like little children. When worldly people consider an awakened being, they will think she's lost it. She doesn't have any interest in the things they live for. To put it another way, an arahant and an insane person are similar. When people look at an arahant, they'll think she's crazy. If you curse her, she doesn't care. Whatever you say to her, she doesn't react, like a crazy person—but crazy and having awareness. A truly insane person may not get angry when she's cursed, but that's because she doesn't know what's going on. Someone observing the arahant and the mad person might see them as the same. But the lowest is mad, living in a condition of intense self-cherishing, while the very highest is the arahant, free of all ideas of and concerns about a self. If you only look at their external manifestations, they may seem similar. But their inner awareness, their sense of things, is very different.

Think about this. When someone says something that ought to make you angry and you just let it go, people might believe you're crazy. So when you teach others about these things, they don't understand very easily. It has to be internalized and experienced directly for them to really understand.

27

My Tooth, My Pillow, My Coconut

WE HEAR THE WORDS of the Dharma, such as, "Nothing is us or ours," and we may think we understand pretty well. When I began practicing, I meditated on the parts of the body and felt I had some insight into anatta and was becoming detached from things. Then one day, I lost a tooth.

"Oh! *My* tooth fell out. It seems I'm getting old." All of a sudden I was melancholy and disheartened.

Later on, I decided to go on *tudong,* ascetic wandering. It's supposed to be the practice of utmost simplicity. Usually you only take your almsbowl and robes and a few essential items, such as a water strainer and needle and thread. I thought I didn't have much attachment to possessions and could be content with little. But when I was putting things together to go, I couldn't bear to leave anything behind. I packed up a huge bag, and it started to look like it would be more than I could carry. Then I thought about my pillow, and I decided I had to have that, too. Everything seemed to be mine, and everything seemed so necessary—even the coconut husk I used to polish the floor.

PART FIVE

POINTS IN MEDITATION

28

Tranquillity and Insight

MEDITATIVE TRANQUILLITY IS USUALLY divided into peace through concentration and peace through wisdom. In peace through concentration, we have to remove ourselves from activity and contact with others. The eye has to be far from sights, the ear far from sounds. Then not hearing, not knowing, and so forth, one can become tranquil. This kind of peacefulness is of value in its way, but it isn't supreme. It is short-lived and unreliable. When the senses meet objects that are pleasing or displeasing, it changes because it is attracted or doesn't want those things to be present. So the mind always has to struggle with these objects, and no wisdom is born, since the meditator always feels that he is not at peace because of those external factors. On the other hand, if you determine not to run away but to look directly at things, you come to realize that lack of tranquillity is not due to external objects or situations, but only happens because of wrong understanding.

When you are intently devoted to finding tranquillity in your meditation, you can seek out the quietest, most remote place, where you won't meet with sights or sounds, where there is nothing going on that will disturb you. There the mind can settle down and become calm because there is nothing to provoke it. Examine this state to see how much strength it has: when you come out of that quiet place and start experiencing sense contact, notice how you become pleased and displeased, gladdened and dejected, and how the mind becomes disturbed. Then you will understand that this kind of tranquillity is not genuine.

Whatever occurs in your field of experience is merely what it is. When something pleases us, we decide that it's good, and when something displeases us, we say it isn't good. That is only our own discriminating minds giving meaning to external objects. Understanding this, we have a basis for investigating these things and seeing them as they really are. When there is tranquillity in meditation, it's not necessary to do a lot of thinking. There is a sensitivity that has a certain knowing quality born of the tranquil mind. This isn't thinking; it's the factor of enlightenment known as investigating Dharma.

This sort of tranquillity doesn't get disturbed by experience and sense contact. But then there is the question, "If it's tranquillity, why is there still something going on?" There is something happening within tranquillity, but it's not something happening in the ordinary way, where we make more out of it than it really is. When something happens within tranquillity, the mind knows it extremely clearly, and wisdom is born. We see the way things actually happen, and then tranquillity becomes all-inclusive. When the eye sees forms or the ear hears sounds, we recognize them for what they are. In this latter form of tranquillity, when the eye sees forms, the mind is peaceful. When the ear hears sounds, the mind is peaceful. Whatever we experience, the mind doesn't waver.

This kind of tranquillity comes from just that other kind of tranquillity, that ignorant concentration. That's the cause that enables it to come about. Wisdom comes from tranquillity, and knowing comes from unknowing; the mind comes to know from that state of unknowing, from learning to investigate like this.

There will be both tranquillity and wisdom, and wherever we are, whatever we are doing, we see the truth. We understand the arising and ceasing of experience in the mind. Then there is nothing more to do, nothing to correct or solve. There is no more speculation and nowhere to go, no escape.

We can only escape through wisdom, knowing things as they are and transcending them. Then we find rest. Once we've practiced to get to the goal, know the goal, and be the goal, then when we are active, there's no way to incur loss or be harmed. When we are sitting still, there is no way we can be harmed. In all situations, nothing can affect us. Practice has matured to fulfillment and we have reached the destination. Maybe today we don't have a chance to sit and practice *samadhi,* meditative stability, but we are OK. Samadhi doesn't mean only sitting. There can be samadhi in all postures. If we are really practicing in all postures we will enjoy samadhi thus. There won't be anything that can interfere. We won't say, "I'm not in a clear state of mind now, so I can't practice." We will never feel that way. This is how practice should be, free of doubt and perplexity.

29

Still Water Flows, Flowing Water Is Still

STILLNESS IS TRANQUILLITY, AND flowing is wisdom. We practice meditation to make the mind calm, like still water. Then it can flow.

In the beginning, we learn what still water is like and what flowing water is like. After practicing for a while, we will see how these two support each other. Both being still and flowing: this is something not easy to contemplate.

We can understand that still water doesn't flow. We can understand that flowing water isn't still. But when we practice we experience both of these together. The mind of a true practitioner is like still water that flows, or flowing water that's still; whatever takes place in the mind of a Dharma practitioner will have that quality. Only flowing is not correct. Only still is not correct. When we have experience of practice, our minds will be in this condition of flowing water that is still.

This is something we've never seen. When we see flowing water, it's just flowing along. When we see still water, it doesn't move. But within our minds, it will really be like this—like flowing water that is still. In our Dharma practice we have samadhi, or tranquillity, and wisdom mixed together. Then, wherever we sit, the mind is still, and it flows. Still, flowing water.

Whenever this occurs in the mind of one who practices, it is something different and strange; it is different from the ordinary mind that one has known all along. Before, when it was moving, it moved. When it was still, it didn't move, but was only still—the mind can be compared to water in this way. But through meditation it enters a condition that is like flowing water being still. Whatever we are doing, the mind is like water that flows yet is still. Making our minds like this, there are both tranquillity and wisdom.

30

Making It Real

THE BUDDHA TAUGHT TO have suitable conditions for living as the support for our meditation practice: a comfortable environment, decent food, good spiritual companions. But good conditions are really not so easy to find. The teachings talk about good conditions like this, but where are they to be found? Wherever we go we don't seem to meet them.

So we wonder, what do we need to be able to practice comfortably? We think that if we had everything just right, good food, a comfortable environment, people around us who speak nicely, we would be all set. Actually, with such wonderful conditions, we might well die of carelessness and indulgence.

People have so many ideas and desires about what constitutes a comfortable situation for practice, but if we have a contented mind that knows moderation, then we can be comfortable anywhere. Staying will be OK. Going will be OK. But for most of us, if we are lacking material requisites, we won't be happy. If there is excess, it becomes difficult. Somehow it's never right. Maybe we don't see eye-to-eye with the way people are doing things, and we will be unhappy over that. Or maybe the teachings we hear don't quite make sense to us.

The Buddha's teaching is correct, but it's our minds that are not yet doing things correctly. People think, "I want to practice samadhi seriously, so I will leave this place. I want to focus exclusively on samadhi practice and really do it." But what does it mean to "really do it"? They don't know if it's real or not. If it's for real, then the mind becomes peaceful! If they are practicing for real, why aren't they at peace yet? This is what to measure by. When it's not "for real" then it's not peaceful.

What does it mean to be really practicing Dharma? There are so many methods of meditation you can practice. It's just like people in the world earning their livelihoods in various ways: there are farmers, businesspeople, civil servants, engineers, factory workers producing all sorts of goods, and it is all summarized as earning a living. Here it's the same for us; we call it practicing Dharma, but the point is that it should be leading you to letting go, to cessation, to making an end of grasping attachment.

31

Serious Students

Ajahn Chah on Intensive Meditation

WHILE AJAHN CHAH INSPIRED great respect in those who lived near him, he didn't want people blindly following him or merely trying to live up to ideals of what they thought meditators should do. He challenged people's thinking, but instead of simply telling them, "No, you're wrong. This is what the Buddha said . . ." he would put the responsibility for their spiritual path back in their hands and allow them the freedom to discover the truth for themselves.

A monk came to Ajahn Chah asking permission to practice on his own for a while, which meant returning to his kuti after the almsround to eat there and meditate in solitude instead of joining the community in the daily routine of taking the meal, chores, chanting services, and meditation. Ajahn Chah, in a severe tone of voice, rhetorically asked, "Do you think you can get away from your defilements that way? Will you become enlightened if you're blind and deaf? We practice with our eyes open here." The monk sat quietly, looking chastised. Then, after a pause and a change of tone, Ajahn Chah said, "OK, give it a try."

Many Westerners who came to Wat Pah Pong thought that they should be meditating as much as possible and not wasting time on group activities such as chanting or sitting through teachings in a language they couldn't understand. One of the first to arrive requested permission to leave the meeting hall after group meditation was over so he could return to his kuti to practice while the others remained for chanting or instruction.

Ajahn Chah, who often spoke of the need for making all activities into meditation, nevertheless agreed to this. Every evening, when the time came, he would announce to the community, "Now the American will go to meditate alone," and an embarrassed monk would get up and walk out.

After a while, he began to feel it was a foolish piece of business, and he decided to surrender to the way of life in the monastery and trust Ajahn Chah to be his teacher, and that was when his meditative awareness really started deepening.

32

Meditation Instructions

Questions and Answers

Student: I'd like to get calmness. I want to meditate and make my mind peaceful.

Ajahn Chah: There you are. You want to get something. If you really want this, you have to consider what it is that causes the mind to not be peaceful. The Buddha taught that everything happens due to causes. But we expect the fruit to just fall into our hands. It's like wanting to eat watermelon without ever planting watermelons. So where will it come from? You only get some once in a while, and then you think, "Oh, it's so sweet, so tasty!" and you want more— "Eh, how can I get more watermelon? Where does it come from? How do people have watermelon to eat?" But it doesn't come from merely speculating about it.

We have to think it through to get the whole picture. Look at all activities of the mind. Having been born into this world, why is it that we have suffering, difficulty, and heaviness? We suffer again and again over the same old things, because our knowledge is not thorough.

What's the problem? We are living with and creating troubles for ourselves, but we don't understand where the difficulty really lies. Living at home, we feel we have difficulties with our spouses, our children, whatever. We talk about it, but we don't truly understand it, so it really is difficult. Struggling to get the mind to samadhi is the same. We can't figure out why we can't realize samadhi. We need to understand the truth of cause and effect, what causes put us in this condition. Everything arises from causes. But we don't get it. It's like having a bottle full of water, then drinking it all and hoping for more—there's no more water that can come out of the bottle. But if we get water from a stream, then we can keep drinking, because the stream keeps providing water.

The stream is like seeing impermanence, unsatisfactoriness, and not-self deeply, knowing it thoroughly. Ordinary, superficial knowledge doesn't know thoroughly, but with penetrating insight, we realize the full depth and flavor of these three characteristics, and then whatever arises, we see the truth of it. When it ceases, we see the truth of that. The mind is always perceiving reality, and with this view, we have arrived at a place of peace, where there is no suffering or difficulty to bear. The problem of grasping onto things and giving them meaning will keep easing up. We see things arise and see them pass away, arising again and ceasing again. Look at this Dharma frequently, contemplate it a lot, develop this awareness a lot. The result will be detachment and dispassion; you become dispassionate about absolutely everything.

The things that contact the ears, eyes, nose, and tongue, the things that are born in the mind, we will comprehend clearly—we will see that they are all the same. Seeing that all these dharmas (phenomena) are of the nature of impermanence, suffering, and not-self, and are not to be grasped even in the slightest, detachment is born. When the eye sees forms or the ear hears sounds, we know them for what they are. When the mind is happy or suffering, when it has reactions of satisfaction or aversion, we know all of these things. If we attach to these things, they stick to us and immediately lead us into becoming. If we release them, they go their way. Let go of sights and they go the way of sights. Let go of sounds and they go the way of all sounds. But when we need to, we can make use of them.

Let things go according to their nature. If we are aware in this way, we will see the fact of impermanence. All phenomena that appear are illusion, without exception; they are all deceptive. But when we recognize that they are deceptions, we can truly be at ease. Having mindfulness and clear comprehension, having wisdom, we don't see anything but this fact that phenomena arise and are of this nature. Even when we are not doing anything in particular, whatever we may be thinking, we will recognize our thoughts as being just like that and won't get caught up in them. If the mind becomes tranquil, we will think, "Tranquil: no big deal. Tranquillity is not permanent." There are only impermanent phenomena, and nothing else. Wherever we sit, Dharma is there, and wisdom arises—what can cause us to suffer then?

We suffer over things that aren't really obtainable, because of thinking things not worth thinking. We have all sorts of desires and want things to be a certain way. Wanting to be anything—such as if you want to be an arahant, a fully enlightened being—is bringing suffering upon yourself. The Buddha taught us to stop wanting to be something, because he realized that all this wanting to get something and to be something is suffering.

⌐⌐⌐

Student: I want to ask for a meditation object that suits my temperament. Sometimes I practice repeating *Buddho* for a long time, but the mind doesn't settle down. I tried meditating on the parts of the body, then I tried recollection of death, but I didn't become tranquil. So I'm at my wit's end as to what to do.

Ajahn Chah: Put it down. When you're at your wit's end, let go.

Student: Sometimes there is some tranquillity, but then memories start coming, a lot of memories, and I get scattered and disturbed again.

Ajahn Chah: There you are: impermanence. Impermanence! All of it is impermanent. Just keep instructing your mind, "Not certain, not sure!" Absolutely all mental phenomena are uncertain; don't forget this point. If the mind is unsettled, that is uncertain. If the mind is peaceful, that is likewise uncertain. Don't grasp either state, and don't take any of these conditions as real. "Consciousness is impermanent." Have you heard this before? Have you studied this? What will you do about it?

Tranquillity is not permanent. Agitation is not permanent. So how will you practice? What view will you take of things? If you have the right understanding, then you recognize these conditions of tranquillity and agitation as unsure things. Then what kind of feeling will you have? Keep looking here.

If your mind becomes peaceful, how many days will that last? If it's disturbed, how many days does that last? Just keep saying, "Not certain!" Then where will things stay? Keep driving them out in this way.

You practice *Buddho* and you're not peaceful. You practice mindfulness of breathing and you're not peaceful. Why are you so attached to the idea of tranquillity? Practice reciting "Buddho, Buddho" and recognize uncertainty. Practice mindfulness of breathing and recognize uncertainty. Don't make such a big deal out of your states of mind, whether peaceful or agitated; they are only going to trick you because of this grasping attachment. We have to be a little more clever than they are. When either condition comes, we know it as uncertain. Then things subside. Try it out. Whatever comes up, keep on remonstrating with it: "Not sure!" Usually we don't oppose or go through it, but instead run right after it.

If someone wants to do a lot of samadhi practice, I applaud that. The teachings speak of liberation through concentration and liberation through wisdom. Liberation means attaining freedom from the taints of craving and ignorance. There are these two types. With liberation through concentration, one develops the power of the mind through samadhi so that wisdom can come about.

Some trees will grow well if you give them a lot of water, but some need only a little water. Like the pine trees here—don't give them too much water or they'll die on you. Some trees grow and bloom with so little water. It can seem strange how they do that.

Meditation practice is similar. In liberation through concentration, you practice meditation strictly, and you need to develop a lot of samadhi. This is one approach, like the trees that need lots of water in order to grow. Then there are the trees that shouldn't have too much water.

So they talk about liberation through concentration and liberation through wisdom, attaining freedom. To attain freedom, of course one has to depend on wisdom and force of mind. The two ways aren't really different. So why are they divided like this? It's just a manner of speaking. If you take it too seriously and try to separate them, it will only make you confused.

Still, they each do have some slight emphasis on one aspect or the other. To call them the same is not right; to say they are different is not right. It's similar to talking about temperament. The teachings mention desire temperament, anger temperament, delusion temperament, and Buddha temperament. It's to indicate which tendencies are stronger than others. They're just terms, something we use to classify. But please don't forget that the point of all our learning and of whatever kind of practice we do is to liberate ourselves through recognizing the impermanent, unsatisfactory, and selfless nature of all phenomena.

⌒

Student: How can we unify concentration practice with discursive meditation, such as contemplating the impermanence of life?

Ajahn Chah: Before we begin, we should sit and let the mind relax. It's similar to doing something like sewing. When we're learning to use the sewing machine, first we just sit in front of the machine to get familiar with it and feel comfortable. If we're going to practice mindfulness of breathing, first we just sit and breathe. Not fixing awareness on anything, we merely take note that we are breathing. We take note of whether the breath is relaxed or not and how long or short it is. Having noticed this, then we begin focusing on the inhalation and exhalation at three points.

We focus attention on the breath as it passes through the nostrils, the chest, and the abdomen. When the air enters, it first passes the nose, then through the chest, then to the end point of the abdomen. As it leaves the body, the beginning is the abdomen, the middle is the chest, and the end is the nose. We merely note it. This is a way to start controlling the mind, tying awareness to these points at the beginning, middle, and end of the inhalations and exhalations.

We practice like this until it's going smoothly. Then the next stage is to focus awareness only on the sensation of the breath at the tip of the nose or the upper lip. At this point we aren't concerned with whether the breath is long or short, but only focus on the sensation of entering and exiting.

There may be different phenomena contacting the senses, or thoughts arising. This is called initial thought (*vitakka*). It brings up some idea, be it about the nature of conditioned phenomena (*sankhara*), about the world, or whatever. Once it appears, the mind will want to get involved and merge with it. If it's an object that is wholesome, then let the mind take it up. If it is something un-wholesome, stop it immediately. If it is something wholesome, let the mind contemplate on it, and gladness and satisfaction will come about. The mind will be bright and clear as the breath goes in and out, these initial thoughts appear, and the mind takes them up. Then it becomes discursive thought (*vicara*). The mind develops familiarity with the object, exerting itself and merging with it.

You're sitting and suddenly the thought of someone pops into your head—that's vitakka, the initial thought. Then you take that idea of the person and start thinking about him in detail. That is vicara. For example, we pick up the idea of death, and then we start considering it: "I will die; others will die; every living being will die; when they die, where will they go . . . ?" Stop! Stop and bring it up again. If it's running away, stop it and go back to mindfulness of the breath. Keep at it until the mind is bright and clear.

Then, as you continue on, there will be the initial thought and discursive thought again and again. If you are contemplating skillfully on an object such as the impermanence of life, then the mind will experience deeper tranquillity, and rapture is born. There is initial and discursive thought, and that leads to the mind being gladdened and enraptured. If you practice vicara with an object that you are suited to, you may experience the hairs of your body standing on end, tears pouring from your eyes, a state of extreme delight—many different things occur as rapture comes.

This rapture will start to diminish and disappear after a while, so you can take up the initial thought again. The mind will become firm and undistracted. Then you go on to discursive thought again, the mind becoming one with it. When you are practicing a meditation that suits your temperament and doing it well, then whenever you take up the object, the mind will become enraptured and satiated. Back and forth between initial and discursive thought, over and over again, rapture comes. Then there is bliss.

This takes place in sitting practice. After sitting for a while, you can get up and do walking meditation. The mind can be the same in the walking. There won't be any of the hindrances of desire, anger, restlessness and agitation, sloth and torpor, or doubt, and the mind will be unstained.

Student: Can this happen with any kind of thinking, or is it in a state of tranquillity that it happens?

Ajahn Chah: It's when the mind is tranquil. It's not ordinary mental proliferation. You sit with a calm mind and then the initial thought comes. For example, I think of my brother, who just passed away. This is when the mind is tranquil—the tranquillity isn't something certain, but for the moment the mind is tranquil. After this initial thought comes, then I go into discursive thought. If it's a line of thinking that's skillful and wholesome, it leads to ease of mind and happiness, and then there is rapture, with its attendant experiences. This rapture comes from the initial and discursive thinking that took place in a state of calmness. We don't have to give it names such as first *jhana* (meditative absorption), second jhana, and so forth. We can just call it tranquillity.

The next factor is bliss. Eventually, we drop the initial and discursive thinking as tranquillity deepens. The state of mind is becoming more refined and subtle. Vitakka and vicara are relatively coarse, and they will vanish. There will remain just the rapture, accompanied by bliss and one-pointedness of mind. And when it reaches full measure, there won't be anything—rapture and bliss fade away, and the mind is empty. That's absorption concentration.

We don't need to fixate or dwell on any of these experiences. They will naturally progress from one to the next. It means the mind is becoming more and more tranquil, and its objects are steadily decreasing, until there is nothing but one-pointedness and equanimity.

When the mind is tranquil and focused, this can happen. It is the power of mind that has attained tranquillity. The hindrances of sensual desire, aversion, doubt, dullness, and restless agitation won't be present. Though they may still exist latent in the mind of the meditator, they won't occur at this time.

The important principle in meditation is not to be in doubt over whatever occurs. Doubt just adds complication. If the mind is bright and awake, don't doubt that. It's a condition of mind. If it's dark and dull, don't doubt about that. Just continue to practice diligently without getting caught up in reactions to those states. Taking note and being aware of them, don't have doubts about them. They are just what they are.

As you do your practice, these states are things you encounter as you progress along. Notice them with awareness, and keep letting go. Whether the mind is dark or illumined, don't fixate on these conditions. Keep walking or sitting, and keep noting what is taking place, without getting bound up or infatuated. Don't make yourself suffer over these conditions of mind. Sometimes the mind will be joyful. Sometimes it will be sorrowful. There can be happiness or suffering. There can be obstruction. Rather than doubting, understand that they are merely impermanent conditions of mind, and that whatever manifests is coming about due to causes ripening. At this moment, this condition is manifesting—that's what you should recognize.

Student: Should we be closing our eyes to shut out the external environment, or should we just deal with things as we see them?

Ajahn Chah: When we are training newly, it's important to avoid too much sensory input, so it's better to close the eyes. Not seeing objects that can distract and affect us, we build up the mind's strength. When the mind is strong, then we can open the eyes, and whatever we see won't sway us. Open or closed won't matter.

When you rest, you normally close your eyes. Sitting in meditation with eyes closed is the dwelling place for a practitioner. We find enjoyment and rest in it. But when we can't close our eyes, will we be able to deal with things? We sit with eyes closed and we profit from that. When we open our eyes, we can handle whatever we meet. Things won't get out of hand—we won't be at a loss. But basically we are just handling things. It's when we go back to our sitting that we really develop greater wisdom.

This is how we develop the practice. When it reaches fulfillment, then whether we open or close our eyes, it will be the same. The mind won't change or deviate. At all times of the day, morning, noon, or night, the state of mind will be the same. There is nothing that can shake the mind. When happiness arises, we recognize, "It's not certain," and it passes. Unhappiness arises and we recognize, "It's not certain," and that's that.

In our meditation we will meet with the arising of all sorts of mental activity and defilements. The correct outlook is to be ready to let go of all of it, whether pleasant or painful. Even though happiness is something we desire and suffering is something we don't desire, we recognize they are of equal value. These are things that we will experience.

Happiness is wished for by people in the world. Suffering is not wished for. Nirvana is something beyond wishing or not wishing. There is no wishing involved in nirvana. Wanting to get happiness, wanting to be free of suffering, wanting to transcend happiness and suffering—there are none of these things. It is peace.

33

What It Is

Ajahn Chah's Meditation

AJAHN CHAH HAD A very direct approach to meditation, and he advised people not to get caught up in doubts or to make too much out of meditative experiences, no matter how unusual or extraordinary they seemed. In an early biography, he described a transformative series of meditative experiences that occurred one night. He felt his body expanding and breaking up, accompanied by loud noises, and when it was over, he asked himself, "What was that?"

The answer came to him immediately: "It was what it was." That settled the matter for him, and it became his approach to meditation and gave an unshakable quality to his practice.

34

Don't Get Drunk on Tranquillity

WHEN I WAS YOUNGER, I looked for peace in the wrong way. I'd sit to practice samadhi, and my mind wouldn't settle down. It ran around wildly, and no matter how I tried to bring it back, it wouldn't return. If it did come back, it wouldn't stay.

What to do? Should I stop breathing? I used to try that. I'd hold my breath to try and force the mind to stop moving. But it would still go. I'd hold the breath longer, but the only thing that could come of holding the breath longer and longer was that I would eventually die.

It was similar when I felt my meditation was disturbed by sounds. I filled my ears with wax. I really stuffed them tight, so that I couldn't hear anything. It seemed like a good thing—no more outside sounds to bother me—but I started thinking about it: If not hearing or seeing anything is the path of the awakened, then the deaf should all be enlightened. The blind should all be enlightened. The completely deaf should be arahants.

So I contemplated this until I got some understanding. I realized that just trying to block things out didn't really protect me, so

I stopped doing that. I realized it was only me and my attachments causing the problems. So now I have a lot of regret. When I think about the way I practiced when I was new to meditation, how deluded I was, I really feel bad. I wanted to practice to be free of suffering, but I was only bringing suffering upon myself, and the result was that there was never any peace for me.

When the mind becomes tranquil, we are delighted. If we have a few days of peace from it, we feel it's really enjoyable. Then one day, all of a sudden it's like sitting on a nest of biting ants. We can't sit, we can't do anything, the mind is so wild and agitated. So we ponder and try to figure out why it isn't like before. It was so peaceful for those few days, and we can't help but long for that experience to return.

Right here we are deluded. Conditions of mind change. They are not fixed, certain, or stable. That is their nature; that is always going to be the way they are. Whatever occurs is already something old; it is not anything different or unique, but is ruled by these same characteristics. We have to keep looking at the mind's reactions, the way it likes some things and dislikes others. When we have liking, we feel pleased, and this sense of being pleased only comes about because of delusion; it's not because we are in the right.

If you are tranquil, don't get drunk on it. If you are distracted, don't get drunk. The Buddha taught not to be intoxicated. This applies to all experience without exception. If we are always wanting more and more, then we are always in a condition of disturbance. The Buddha thus said that there is no wisdom in mere *samatha,* tranquillity meditation. In this samatha practice, first we may be tranquil because we are separated from external sense objects. Not hearing sounds, not experiencing the objects of the other senses, we can become peaceful. That's good in its own way. It's because we've escaped from things for a while. It's like certain illnesses, such as cancer. It may not be noticeable for some time; there are no symptoms, such as pain or swelling, so the person feels OK as long as the disease hasn't manifested. That's being in samatha and not noticing anything, feeling one has no defilement. But when we leave that tranquil environment and start encountering sights and sounds, we may be disturbed by those things. So then what can you do? Where can you stay in this world? Where can you go that you won't see, hear, smell, taste, or have physical contact with anything?

The Buddha wanted our eyes to see things, our ears to hear sounds, our noses to know smells, our tongues to experience tastes, our bodies to feel hard and soft, cold and hot. He wanted us to have this full range of experience, not to live in total isolation. He wanted us to experience these things and realize, "Aha! This is the way things are." This is how we can come to wisdom. Even if we aren't doing sitting and walking meditation all the time, the mind can still be aware and on track, practicing energetically without there being any loss or deterioration. One who is skillful practices Dharma in this way.

Have you seen the old meditation masters? They're indifferent to things. We can't really understand their equanimity. It's because their minds are cool and they have knowledge. Whenever suffering tries to approach, it doesn't shake them. When happiness comes, it doesn't shake them. "Don't bother me, little child!" That's how they view these things. When unhappiness comes—"Don't bother me, little child!" They are adults; the defilements can only sit around helplessly. We look at them and wonder how they can be like that. Our own minds heat up over such things. So it's taught that we should find an accomplished spiritual teacher and take his or her example as a foundation, contemplating it over a long period of time.

35

Keep At It

Little by little, we can work at meditation. We don't have deep knowledge yet; we don't really know what we're doing, but we can progress a little at a time. We may not know that we benefit from it, but we do, little by little. When you eat your food, are you full after the first mouthful? You won't feel that way. But you could say you're full, though not very full. Take the second mouthful, and you're more full, but still it's just a little. If you keep on eating, a little at a time, you will get there. Think about it, look ahead, and you will see where you are going: finally you will be slowly chewing your last mouthful. Small things accumulate, and hunger is reduced, until finally you will be full—maybe to the point where you can't look at any more food. The mouthfuls you have eaten, one at a time, have filled you.

Old folks here will tell you there's fire in dry bamboo. In the past, matches were hard to come by and didn't always work. When people went into the forest, they could just find some dry wood, and they knew there was fire in it. Whenever they wanted to cook, they only had to rub two pieces of dry bamboo together to start a fire. They would just keep rubbing them together. At first the wood was cold. Rubbing for a while, it got hot, then after some time there was smoke. But it did take a while to get hot, and even more time to make smoke and finally fire.

Now we, their children and descendants in these times, don't have much patience. If we try to rub pieces of bamboo to make fire, within two minutes we're getting restless. We get fed up and put the sticks down: "Time to take a break!" Then when we pick them up again, we find they're cold. We start rubbing once more, but we're starting from the beginning again so they don't get hot very quickly, and again we get impatient. Like this, we could keep at it for an hour or a whole day and wouldn't see any fire. We rub and stop, rub and stop. Then we start to criticize the old people: "These old-timers are crazy. I don't know what they're talking about. They must be lying. I've been rubbing the sticks all this time and still there's nothing."

This is what happens if our understanding and commitment to practice don't go far enough. There's not enough heat, but we expect to have fire. The old folks have done that, but they know it takes some effort. You have to keep rubbing without taking a break; if you take a break, you only get cold sticks.

It's like the students who travel here to study meditation. They listen to some teaching and they want to get it fast. They want to find the method of meditation that will give them results fastest of all. I tell them, "If you want 'fastest' it won't work." There's such a thing as cause and result; the results will be born of the appropriate causes. It doesn't simply appear in an instant as we desire it to. "Fastest"—even the Buddha would be stumped.

We will progress on the path because of continuous effort, just like someone rubbing pieces of bamboo to get fire. Rubbing without stopping, the heat increases. The more she rubs, the hotter it gets. When smoke appears, fire is near; but at the point when she gets smoke, she doesn't take a break. It's not a game, so she knows she has to keep at it. In that way she gets fire.

36

High Ideals and Daily Frustrations

A Young Monk with Ajahn Chah

A YOUNG MONK WHO had fancied himself an able meditator when he first arrived at Wat Pah Pong told of meeting Ajahn Chah. He related his experiences with different meditation teachers, feeling that he must be making quite an impression on the master. Ajahn Chah didn't say a word, but instead left his seat, got down on all fours, and started sniffing around like a dog. The young man realized that Ajahn Chah might be trying to tell him something.

He stayed and undertook the training, and before long began to feel that he was accomplishing nothing and that life itself was devoid of joy or meaning. Convinced he would never smile again, he went to see Ajahn Chah.

Ajahn Chah told him, "You're like a baby squirrel. It sees the adults climbing trees and jumping from branch to branch, and it wants to do that. So it crawls out on a limb and loses its balance, and bam! It hits the ground. The mother picks it up and brings it back to the tree, but it still wants to run and jump. Off it goes again, and bam! It falls again." Ajahn Chah continued the tale, with the poor little squirrel hitting the ground over and over, until the monk who'd thought he would never smile again was literally rolling on the floor of the kuti in laughter.

Later he was again becoming disheartened over his inability to live up to the high ideals he held about monastic life and meditation despite all his efforts to follow the rules and practice hard. He went to see Ajahn Chah to express his frustration. Ajahn Chah told him a story.

"There was once a donkey who used to listen to the crickets sing. The donkey thought, 'How wonderful to be able to sing like that!' He asked the other animals what the crickets' secret was, and they told him that the crickets drink dew.

"So every morning he went around licking the dew on the grass, and finally one day he opened his mouth to sing. But he still brayed like a donkey."

PART SIX

COMPLETING
THE PATH

37

Making an End of Problems

WHATEVER THE VARIOUS DISPOSITIONS of people may be, whatever desire, aversion, delusion, or pride they may have, the Buddha taught how to practice to reduce these things and eventually make an end of them. This is the best kind of knowledge. In the disciplines of worldly knowledge, various people study various things and gain various sorts of knowledge. Some attain to higher positions and then consider themselves important. The result is that people can't get along, and society becomes inharmonious. This is the way of external knowledge and disciplines.

In the Buddhist way, we are willing to listen to the truth of things and try to gain understanding of what is true and correct. What's the point of that? It is for resolving our problems. Our practice of Dharma is for resolving all those problems we experience in the world, both our own and others' problems, family problems, any kind of the many and difficult problems people face these days.

There are many sorts of problems, but the Buddha taught the real and ultimate way to solve them. The real fact of the matter, the true solution, is that there is no one to solve problems, and there are no problems: there's no one to solve problems, so those problems don't actually exist. This is where it should end up. If there is someone solving problems, there are going to be lots of problems, and there won't be any end to it—that's the way of the world.

In the way of Dharma, we say there is no one to solve problems, and there are no problems. That's how we can make an end of it; that is the way to peace. If there is someone solving problems, there will always be problems. If we perceive problems, then there is someone solving problems.

To give a small example, in the past, conditions were pretty simple here. We rarely had floods because there were no dams. Now, poverty has become a concern. People can't grow enough food, so the rivers are dammed everywhere. A lot of trees have been lost. When there's heavy rain, the water overflows the dams, so it has to be released, and the villages and towns below are flooded. In the past, we let nature be as it is, and water flowed evenly, without flooding. Like this, when there is progress, some kind of loss follows. If nothing is done, people suffer from poverty and want. If steps are taken to alleviate it, some other troubles spring up. The world is like this; there is no way to resolve things once and for all and make an end of it. The condition in which things can come to an end is when there are no problems and no one to solve problems. Finished!

What should we do? Being born into this world, we all face a lot of difficulty. With so many beings existing in the world together, there is bound to be discord and confusion. The Buddha said that when there are problems, there is someone to solve them, and when there is someone to solve problems, there will always be problems. When there is birth, there will be death.

Most of us are in favor of birth. We don't need to seek death, because it automatically comes along with birth. They are two sides of the same thing. No matter how much we don't wish to have death, it's always following along. That's a fact of nature. But it's hard to accept. We have the feeling, "I'm happy about being born, but I don't wish to die." Or, if we have to die, let others die first, and we will go afterward. Let us live as long as possible. But won't that be a lot of suffering, to live so long, ninety years or more? We have this idea that living very long will bring happiness. That's really deluded thinking. It's like in and out breath. If you think being born without dying would be so great, then try stopping your breath after you inhale.

Which one has more value, breathing in or breathing out? Think about it. It's just like being born and dying. If you say inhaling is more important, then try to only inhale without exhaling. How many minutes will you last? Or if you think exhaling is more important, try exhaling and not inhaling again.

To me, the teaching of the Buddha is just right. He recognizes the continuity of birth and death, birth and death. And he says, "That one who sees emptiness, the Lord of Death cannot follow." Death will not affect us then. Why is that? Because there is no "us."

This aggregation that is sitting here the Buddha called *khandhas*, or "heaps"—the heap of bodily form, the heap of feeling, the heap of perception, the heap of thoughts, the heap of consciousness. That's what a human being is. There are only these five heaps. Where is the person? The person is merely imputed on the collection of earth, water, fire, and air; these elements are conventionally thought of as a person. The Lord of Death cannot follow after and find the person. He can only follow after the elements of earth, water, fire, and air that break up and disperse. There is no person to be found therein.

When we recognize that the body is empty, then we don't dwell in it, and the Lord of Death cannot catch us. We don't die! Isn't that right? We don't die when there is no "we," when there is no self. The Buddha talked about anatta, lack of a self. But when you hear this, please listen clearly. In the real meaning of anatta, where is there a person? There are heaps of earth, water, fire, and air—emptiness. Though things are empty, we make conventions to designate that this is me and this is mine, and so self-grasping comes about. Then when earth, water, fire, and air break up, we die, because we have established ourselves there. Those things are not empty to us, rather they are self, and so we must die, and we must grieve and shed tears over death. The Buddha taught that there are merely elements. Our being born is merely the coming together of the elements. When the elements break up, death does not affect us, because we don't dwell in those things.

Think about a grub that becomes a bee. When the bee emerges, it leaves an empty shell behind. Where is the bee? When we look at the shell, we don't know. The bee doesn't dwell there anymore.

So the Buddha taught to remove concepts of self. If we understand the convention of self and the reality of not-self, then problems are finished. It's not really that problems are finished, but that there is no need for solutions. There are no problems because there is no one to solve problems. If we clearly see this, then our lives become free of struggle and contention.

The Buddha taught to contemplate *sankhara,* the impermanent phenomena of body and mind, to know them for what they are. This is wisdom, and this is how our view comes to be free of attachment to self. To state it simply, we can talk like this: there is no one who dies. If we remove the grasping at a self from these things, then there will only be the collapse of earth, water, fire, and air.

There is a story of the venerable Sariputta, one of the Buddha's foremost disciples, instructing the monk Gunamantani. Gunamantani was a student of Sariputta who was preparing to go on ascetic wandering (*tudong*).

Gunamantani felt he was all set to go. But when one goes on tudong, one meets with all sorts of obstacles and situations. As his teacher, Sariputta wanted to check the extent of his disciple's knowledge before he set out on his own; he wanted to find out if Gunamantani was genuinely prepared for it. Sariputta questioned him, "Should there be some person, such as a sage or ordinary householder, who asks you, 'Venerable Gunamantani, when enlightened beings pass away, where are they reborn?' how will you answer them?"

The venerable Gunamantani replied, "I will say to them, 'Form, feeling, perception, thought, and consciousness appear and then cease to be.'"

I read this when I was in my studies, and it didn't make any sense to me. One person is asking one thing, the other is replying about something else, and the two don't seem to meet at all. Of course, it really does make sense, the reply really does answer the question in the most genuine way; it's just that I was too ignorant to understand. When Gunamantani was asked what becomes of the *ariya* who passes away, he didn't say directly. He only answered that "form, feeling, perception, thought, and consciousness, having appeared, then cease to be," because such persons do not die. There are merely the aggregates appearing and disappearing. They don't dwell there. They don't die or take birth. That's all there is to the matter. There's no answer because there's no real question or problem and no one to solve the problem. It all ends with this.

Do you understand how things end? They end with there being nothing. But if someone talks about having nothing or there being nothing, we really become disheartened—after all, we do have a lot of possessions. What about all the things we have at home? But you should be careful about this. Don't get too anxious about the things you own; they aren't really yours.

We can't get this point. We may want to understand it, but it's so hard. We listen and ponder, it may seem right and we sort of understand, but we can't quite get it. The mental defilements are thick, and they obstruct us.

Greed binds us tightly. Hearing about being of few wishes, for example, is not at all satisfying to people. They are of many wishes and want so much and generally won't stop until they're in over their heads and have come to grief. They're going in a different direction from the Dharma altogether.

So we need to listen to the Buddha's teachings carefully. He taught the Dharma for people to transcend suffering, to live free of suffering. If there is no suffering, what will that be like? There will be no self, no me and mine. But there should be wisdom at work in this "no me and mine" so that benefit comes about. For example, if we say, "This body is not mine," and then take a weapon to destroy it, that doesn't bring any benefit. "These cups and dishes aren't mine, so I might as well smash them all and get rid of them"—that's the most ignorant sort of person. Or when you're feeling burdened by having children, you might think, "Well, the teachings say these children aren't really mine, so I can abandon them." Don't do that!

If there is no self, then how can there be anything belonging to a self? Think about this well. It should be obvious. If there is "me," then there are things belonging to "me." This glass then becomes mine. If there is no me, then the glass isn't mine. When something breaks or is lost, it's as if you're watching someone else's possession breaking or being lost, and there won't be the level of distress you would have if it were yours. It all depends on whether or not there is the concept of self involved. So we are told to destroy this mass of self, to destroy it with wisdom—we can't destroy it by stabbing and burying it. The aim of the Buddha is to know the world fully. If we know it well, there won't be any difficulty, because we won't be carrying the world. But without knowledge, we carry absolutely everything.

People these days are like someone trying to fill a water barrel without pouring the water into the opening. They pour it all around, so it doesn't go in and fill the barrel. They could pour water for a year or a lifetime without filling it that way. People's desires in the present time are like that. They are constantly in search of more and are never satisfied.

The poor are full of desires, craving more. The rich are also full of desires and craving more. It's gotten to the point where we can't find any rich people; everyone is impoverished by their desires. Wanting brings us such immense suffering. It's something we really ought to investigate and reflect on.

I've been teaching and training people almost thirty years now. I feel that the point of it is for people to at least realize the Dharma, to relieve their burden and not have to stay too long. If at the least you can enter the stream to enlightenment and ensure there won't be an eighth rebirth, that would be pretty good. Don't let yourselves be born in miserable forms such as fleas and lice, or as turtles, pigs, and dogs, as deaf and blind people, or other kinds of unfortunate beings. We don't have any idea where we might end up if we don't escape now.

The aim of our study and practice is simply so that we don't have to suffer. No suffering. It means suffering cannot find us. The Lord of Death cannot find us.

There are physical form, feelings, perceptions, thought, and consciousness. They appear and disappear; there is no person there, only impermanent, unreliable phenomena. If you think that you die, then you will be reborn here and there, again and again. You will suffer with no end, because it's not finished.

The Conqueror (the Buddha) is one who is finished. Finished in all ways, finished with everything. But if we talk about "finished," people are uncomfortable. They think there will be no place for them to live anymore. They hear talk of finished, done with, nothing, and not understanding it, they can't see that it will be a state of happiness and ease.

It's something difficult to get across. We talk about the supramundane, transcending the world—transcending all the habits, views, thinking, and feeling of people in the world. The mundane means being of the world. Whatever we may gain or accomplish in the world, it is still of the world and subject to decay and loss, so don't get too carried away by it. It's like a beetle scratching at the earth. It can scratch up a pile that's a lot bigger than itself, but it's still only a pile of dirt. If it works hard, it makes a deep hole in the ground, but it's only a hole in dirt. If a buffalo drops a load of dung there, it will be bigger than the beetle's pile of earth, but it still isn't anything that reaches to the sky. It's all dirt. Worldly accomplishments are like this. No matter how hard the beetles work, they're just involved in dirt, making holes and piles.

People who have good worldly karma have the intelligence to do well in the world. But no matter how well they do, they're still living in the world. All the things they do are worldly and have their limits, like the beetle scratching away at the earth. The hole may go deep, but it's in the earth. The pile may get high, but it's just a pile of dirt. Doing well, getting a lot, we're just doing well and getting a lot in the world.

Worldly knowledge and accomplishments on whatever level still leave you in this realm of suffering. Whatever happiness there may be comes about in dependence on external things. It's not the happiness of freedom, the happiness that doesn't depend on anything external. What is it that we depend on? We depend on possessions, on pleasure, on reputation, on praise, on wealth. We lean on all these things, like leaning on a rotting old tree trunk. After we lean for too long, it breaks and falls, and we fall with it. Such is worldly happiness. But the Buddha wanted us to know about it. You live among these things, so be aware of what they are.

Poison is dangerous when someone swallows it. Otherwise, no matter how strong the poison may be, it's not a danger to the person who knows what it is and doesn't swallow it.

The person who makes the poison feels it's good—but it's good in a bad way. She wants to sell it, so she has to promote it: "This mixture is very good indeed! If you give it to a rat, the rat will die. Give it to a dog and the dog will die. It kills whatever you give it to. It can kill chickens, ducks, and people too! That's how good my product is!"

"Well, if it's so good, why don't you take it?"

"Oh no, I won't take it."

"Why not?"

"It's good for killing people and animals. It's not for me to take."

"Good" that is outside of the Dharma is like that, only good to such an extent. The person who promotes her poison as being so great won't take it herself. She talks about it being something really good, but she knows it kills, and she loves her own life. There are many things that people call good. But the Dharma of the Buddha is something that is complete and without harm. It is well explained and full of reason. Still, when people meet it and try to understand, they encounter difficulty, because they are obstructed by self-grasping. But if you can let go as we've been talking about, then the burden of lust, anger, and delusion in your lives will lighten.

If you can realize that there are merely the aggregates and the elements, and that a "person" is just imputed on them, if you really see this clearly, then whatever anyone says, it won't matter much to you. If you're slandered or insulted, you'll be fine. But someone who doesn't understand won't likely feel too fine about it. He'll have to clench his teeth and work really hard to restrain himself.

If we really accept the Dharma like this, then we won't be beset with problems. We won't need to solve problems; they will be resolved of themselves. Why is this world a place of difficulty? It's because we want to follow our inclinations and have things our own way, and we want everything to be just so. But things can't always be as we wish; that's just how it is. We have ideas about the way we want people and situations to be. So we are bothered and offended by things.

Husband and wife don't have peace of mind because they feel bothered and upset by their children. They feel bothered by each other. They feel bothered by the dog and the cat. They are bothered by their work. They are bothered by friends and neighbors. With this sense of being bothered, fear and anxiety are always present. And so they suffer.

Where will you live? If you want everyone's speech and behavior to be agreeable, where can you stay in this world? All you will get with such an attitude is a living death of endless suffering. If we depend on others to speak and act in ways that are always pleasing to us, can we ever be happy? Even for one couple living together, just about every day they will have some disagreement and get upset with each other, if not a lot, then a little. If you think the way to happiness is that no one says anything disagreeable to you, you won't find anywhere to stay in this world. It's living death; we meet with suffering day after day. We want to be happy, but how will we find happiness if our outlook isn't in harmony with reality?

So where can we escape from suffering? I'll give this to all of you for homework. Consider it carefully. You row a boat across a river. You have to row hard to get across, but once you've crossed it's still not over if you're not clever. If you are still carrying the boat as you go through the forest you'll be bumping into the trees.

I'm offering this to you to embellish your understanding. Those who don't realize the Dharma, though they study Dharma and understand Dharma, are still not free. If you have only learned, understood, and practiced the Dharma, don't start dreaming that you are done; your tears will still be flowing. If we *are* Dharma, then we just see heaps of earth, water, fire, and air. Well, we're pretty far from this, aren't we? This is not just joking around.

I'm saying these things for those of you who want to get the essence of the Dharma. The point isn't merely having a comfortable life as your reward for good works. That way you're still building bridges and roads to take rebirth here and there. That way is still full of troubles. Today I'm speaking bluntly and directly. Anyone who doesn't have the right outlook will feel like his neck is being broken. This is the Dharma for grownups.

People have so many desires. But in the end, the place we have to get to is where everything is done with, finished, gotten rid of. We don't get rid of it by throwing it in the river; we finish it with wisdom. Then we live happily and at ease, without suffering. We don't suffer in our work, we don't suffer in our relations with others. We don't suffer when we fall ill—we recognize that there is only earth, water, fire, and air. There are no problems and no one to solve problems. It's finished like that.

38

Seeking a Teacher

Ajahn Chah and a Would-Be Student

A MEDITATION MONK FROM southern Thailand who was considered a master in his own right went to see Ajahn Chah and asked to become his disciple. But Ajahn Chah merely told him, "If you seek a teacher, you won't find a teacher. If you have a teacher, you have no teacher. If you stay with me, you won't see me. If you give up the teacher, you will find the teacher."

Brought up short, somewhat disappointed but still trusting that Ajahn Chah was a man of superior wisdom, the monk paid his respects and went into the forest to contemplate these words. Meditating through the night, he finally realized Ajahn Chah was telling him that the real Dharma is to be found within each individual's heart, and just this Dharma is the true teacher. In the morning, he presented his understanding. Ajahn Chah gave his approval, and the monk returned to his monastery, feeling that he had fulfilled his purpose in going to see Ajahn Chah.

39

A Wise Crab

THERE WAS ONCE A large pond full of fish. As time passed, the rainfall decreased and the pond became shallow. One day a bird showed up at the edge of the pond. He told the fish, "I really feel sorry for you fish. Here you barely have enough water to keep your backs wet. Do you know that not very far from here there's a big lake, several yards deep, where the fish swim happily?"

When the fish in that shallow pond heard this, they got excited. They said to the bird, "It sounds good. But how could we get there?"

The bird said, "No problem. I can carry you in my bill, one at a time."

The fish discussed it among themselves. "It's not so great here anymore. The water doesn't even cover our heads. We ought to go." So they lined up to be taken by the bird.

The bird took one fish at a time. As soon as he got out of sight of the pond, he landed and ate the fish. Then he would return to the pond and tell them, "Your friend is right this moment swimming happily in the lake, and he asks when you will be joining him!"

It sounded great to the fish. They couldn't wait to go, and they started pushing to get to the head of the line.

The bird finished off the fish like that. He went back to the pond to see if he could find any more, but there was only one crab. The bird started his sales pitch about the lake.

The crab was somewhat skeptical. He asked the bird how he could get there. The bird told him he would carry him in his bill. But this crab had wisdom. He told the bird, "Let's do it like this: I'll sit on your back, with my arms around your neck. If you try any tricks, I'll choke you with my claws."

The bird was frustrated by this, but he gave it a try, thinking he might still somehow get to eat the crab. So the crab got on his back, and they took off.

The bird flew around, looking for a good place to land. But as soon as he tried to descend, the crab started squeezing his throat with his claws. The bird couldn't even cry out—he just made a dry, croaking sound. So in the end he had to give up and return the crab to the pond.

If you are like those fish, you will listen to the voices that tell you how wonderful everything can be if only you would go back to worldly ways. It's an obstacle we meet with on the path. So I hope you can be wise, like the crab.

40

Some Final Advice

WHEN THE MIND IS untrained, we tend to believe only in our own likes and dislikes. What we like is good, and what we dislike is bad. We may even decide that harmful things are good. And it's true, but only for our own unreliable, changeable minds; it has nothing to do with Dharma, and it is not true in the light of reality.

So it's taught that we should yank the mind toward the Dharma, to enter the Dharma. Don't try to yank the Dharma toward the mind. Just as in the customs of society, a lesser, ordinary person will go to seek out an important person—the important person doesn't need to go to see the ordinary person. If we want to accomplish the Buddha's way, we should be willing to seek out the Buddha and his teaching and submit to them. We don't expect the Buddha to come and submit to his students. This is a time-honored way.

Just because you like something, will you decide that it is good and right? It's good only because of your habits. That's the confused view of an untrained mind. So before the mind is well trained, we have to push it toward the Dharma and gradually make it accord with Dharma. Eventually the mind is Dharma and Dharma is the mind. Then all activities are Dharma. Thinking is Dharma. Everything we do is Dharma; it is truth.

Once a tortoise and a snake lived in a forest. The forest was on fire, and they were trying to flee. The tortoise was lumbering along, and then it saw the snake slither by. It felt pity for that snake. Why? The snake had no legs, so the tortoise figured it wouldn't be able to escape the fire. It wanted to help the snake. But as the fire kept spreading, the snake fled easily, while the tortoise couldn't make it, even with its four legs, and it died there.

That was the tortoise's ignorance. It thought, if you have legs, you can move. If you don't have legs, you can't go anywhere. So it was worried about the snake. It thought the snake would die because it didn't have legs. But the snake was cool about it; it wasn't worried, because it could easily escape the danger.

This is one way to talk to people with confused ideas. They will feel pity for you and consider you ignorant if you aren't like them and don't have their views and their knowledge. But who is really ignorant?

People may look at you and feel that your way of life, your interest in Dharma, makes no sense. Others may say that if you want to practice Dharma, you ought to ordain. Ordaining or not ordaining isn't the crucial point. It's how you practice.

Laypeople live in the realm of sensuality. They have families, money, and possessions, and are deeply involved in all sorts of activities. Yet sometimes they will gain insight and see Dharma before monks and nuns do. Why is this? It's just because of their suffering from all these things. They see the fault and can let go. They can put it down after seeing clearly in their experience. Seeing the harm and letting go, they are then able to make good use of their positions in the world and benefit others.

We ordained people, on the other hand, might sit here daydreaming about lay life, thinking how great it could be. "Oh yeah, I'd work my fields and make money, then I could have a nice family and a comfortable home." We don't know what it's really like. The laypeople are out there doing it, breaking their backs in the fields, struggling to earn some money and survive. But for us, it's only fantasy.

The laypeople live in a certain kind of thoroughness and clarity. Whatever they do, they really do it. Even getting drunk, they do it thoroughly and have the experience of what it actually is, while we can only imagine what it's like. So, because of their experience, they may become tired of things and realize the Dharma quicker than monks can.

One should be one's own witness. Don't take others as your witness. It means learning to trust yourself. People may think you're crazy, but never mind. It only means they don't know anything about Dharma. But if you lack confidence and instead rely on the opinions of unenlightened people, you can easily be deterred. In Thailand these days, it's hard for young people to sustain an interest in Dharma. Maybe they come to the monastery a few times, and then their friends start teasing them: "Hey, Dhamma Dhammo!" They start changing their ways, no longer seeing value in seeking fun, and their friends complain: "Since you started going to the monastery, you don't want to hang out or go drinking anymore. What's wrong with you?" So they often give up the path.

Others' words can't measure your practice. And you don't realize the Dharma because of what others say. I mean the real Dharma. The teachings others can give you are to show you the path, but that isn't real knowledge. When people genuinely meet the Dharma, they realize it directly within themselves. So the Buddha said that he is merely the one who shows the way. In teaching us, he is not accomplishing the way for us. It's not so easy as that. It's like someone who sells us a plow to till the fields. He isn't going to do the plowing for us. We have to do that ourselves. Don't wait for the salesman to do it. Once he's made the sale, he takes the money and splits. That's his part.

That's how it is in practice. The Buddha shows the way. He's not the one who does it for us. Don't expect that salesman to till your field. If we understand the path in this way, it's a little more comfortable for us, and we will do it ourselves. Then there will be fruition.

━◦━

Teachings can be most profound, but those who listen may not understand. But never mind. Don't be perplexed over profundity or lack of it. Just do the practice wholeheartedly, and you can arrive at real understanding—it will bring you to the place the teachings talk about.

Don't rely on the perceptions of ordinary people. Have you read the story about the blind men and the elephant? It's a good illustration. Suppose there's an elephant, and a group of blind people are trying to describe it. One touches the leg and says it's like a pillar. Another touches the ear and says it's like a fan. Another touches the tail and says, "No, it's not a fan, it's like a broom." Another touches the body and says it's something else again from what the others say.

There's no resolution. Each blind person touches part of the elephant and has a completely different idea of what it is. But it's the same one elephant. It's like this in practice. With a little understanding or experience, you get limited ideas. You can go from one teacher to the next seeking explanations and instructions, trying to figure out if they are teaching correctly or incorrectly and how their teachings compare to each other. Some people are always traveling around to learn from different teachers. They try to judge and measure, so when they sit down to meditate they are constantly in confusion about what is right and what is wrong. "This teacher said this, but that teacher said that. One guy teaches in this way, but the other guy's methods are different. They don't seem to agree." It can lead to a lot of doubt.

You might hear that certain teachers are really good, and so you go to receive teachings from Thai ajahns, Zen masters, vipassana teachers, and others. It seems to me that most of you have probably had enough teaching, but the tendency is to always want to hear more, to compare, and to end up in doubt as a result. Each successive teacher might well increase your confusion further.

Thus the Buddha said, "I am enlightened through my own efforts, without any teacher." A wandering ascetic asked him, "Who is your teacher?" The Buddha answered, "I have no teacher. I attained enlightenment by myself." But that wanderer just shook his head and went away. He thought the Buddha was making up a story and had no interest in what he said. He believed it wasn't possible to achieve anything without a teacher and guide.

You study with a spiritual teacher, and she tells you to give up greed and anger. She tells you they are harmful and that you need to get rid of them. Then you may practice and do that. But getting rid of greed and anger doesn't come about just because she taught you; you have to actually practice and accomplish that. Through practice you come to realize something for yourself. You see greed in your mind and give it up. You see anger in your mind and give it up. The teacher doesn't get rid of them for you. She tells you about getting rid of them, but it doesn't happen just because she tells you. You do the practice and come to realization. You understand these things for yourself.

It's like the Buddha is catching hold of you and bringing you to the beginning of the path, and he tells you, "Here is the path— walk on it." He doesn't help you walk. You do that yourself. When you do travel the path and practice Dharma, you meet the real Dharma, which is beyond anything that anyone can explain to you. So one is enlightened by oneself, understanding past, future, and present, understanding cause and result. Then doubt is finished.

We talk about giving up and developing, renouncing and cultivating. But when the fruit of practice is realized, there is nothing to add and nothing to remove. The Buddha taught that this is the point we want to arrive at, but people don't want to stop there. Their doubts and attachments keep them on the move, keep them

confused, keep them from stopping. So when one person has arrived but others are somewhere else, they won't be able to make
any sense of what he may say about it. They might have some
intellectual understanding of the words, but this is not real knowledge of the truth.

Usually when we talk about practice we talk about what to
develop and what to renounce, about increasing the positive and
removing the negative. But the final result is that all of these are
done with. There is the level of *sekha,* the person who needs to
train in these things, and there is the level of *asekha,* the person who
no longer needs to train in anything. When the mind has reached
the level of full realization, there is nothing more to practice. Such
a person doesn't have to make use of any of the conventions of
teaching and practice. It's spoken of as someone who has gotten rid
of the defilements.

The sekha person has to train in the steps of the path, from the
very beginning to the highest level. When she has completed this,
she is called asekha, meaning she no longer needs to train, because
everything is finished. The things to be trained in are finished.
Doubts are finished. There are no qualities to be developed. There
are no defilements to remove. This is talking about the empty
mind. Once this is realized, you will no longer be affected by whatever good or evil there is. You are unshakable no matter what you
meet, and you live in peace and happiness.

~

In this realm of impermanence, there will be times when we
cannot find spiritual teachers to point out the path to us. Then,
after some time, such teachers on occasion appear. This isn't something we can always count on. And when there is no spiritual guidance for people, we become thickly obscured by craving, and
society in general is ruled by desire, anger, and delusion. So at the
present time, though the Buddhist religion may be struggling to
survive, though in general the way it's practiced is far from the truth

of what it really is, we should make the most of the opportunity we do have.

When the Buddha passed into final nirvana, the different types of disciples had different feelings. There were those who had awakened to the Dharma, and when they saw the Buddha enter nirvana, they were happy: "The Lord Buddha is well-gone; he has gone to peace." But those whose defilements were not yet finished thought, "The Buddha has died! Who will teach us now? The one we bowed down before is gone!" So they wailed and shed tears. That's really bad, crying over the Buddha, like a bunch of bums. Thinking like fools, they feared no one would teach them anymore. But those who were awakened understood that the Buddha is just this Dharma that he has taught us; though he passes away, his teachings are still here. So their spirits were still strong, and they did not lack for means of practice because they understood that the Buddha does not die.

We can easily see that except for the Dharma, there is nothing that will relieve the trouble and distress in the world and cool the fires of beings' torment. Ordinary people of the world are struggling, fighting, suffering, and dying in their lives of ignorance, without any end in sight, because they are not following a true spiritual path. So let's make efforts to devote our minds and bodies to discovering virtue and spirituality, to becoming real human beings who live according to the Dharma of humans. We don't have to look at others and be critical of their lack of virtue. Even when those close to us can't practice, we should do what we can first. Before we worry about the deficiencies of others, those of us who understand and can practice should do that straight away.

Outside of the Dharma, there isn't anything that will bring peace and happiness to this world. Outside of Dharma, there is only the struggle of winning and losing, envy and ill will. One who enters the Dharma lets go of these things and spreads loving kindness and compassion instead. Even a little bit of such Dharma is of great benefit. Whenever an individual has such qualities in the heart, the Buddha's way is flourishing.

Translator's
Acknowledgments

THIS BOOK COULD NEVER have been published without the guidance of Emily Bower, my editor at Shambhala Publications. She was merciless in her appraisals of early drafts, refused to let me get away with vagueness, and over the course of a year patiently steered me to create something coherent, all the while fighting my inertia, stubborn dislike of rewriting, and pride in what I thought of as my brilliance. Dave O'Neal and Peter Turner offered their helpful suggestions through her.

The Sangha of Ajahn Chah's disciples, especially at Abhayagiri Monastery, supplied encouragement, feedback, and help in translation. Abhayagiri was the audience for first drafts, and the monks, nuns, and lay practitioners there always showed boundless appreciation for every little bit of Ajahn Chah's teaching that I was able to translate. The monastery also provided a CD of photographs, which were reformatted by Ruth Stiles of the Sati Center for Buddhist Studies. Ajahn Pasanno, co-abbot of Abhayagiri, has always been my most valuable and reliable resource for questions on translation, Dharma, and scripture.

Other photos were offered by Mr. George Sharp, who was instrumental in bringing Ajahn Chah's monastic tradition to the West, and Venerable Ajahn Munindo of Aruna Ratanagiri Monastery, England.

Bill Sand is an old friend who miraculously reappeared after more than thirty years and gave me invaluable insight into the rewriting process. My "focus group," consisting of Bill, Cathy Colclough, Iris Landsberg, Becca Titus, and Sean Hoade, helped me to understand how to make the teachings more accessible to others.

The National Association of Letter Carriers provided the living wage that paid the bills while I translated. In addition to being indefatigably patient and supportive, my wife, Lili, also rescued me with tech support and an occasional edit, and our unique and amazing dog Bear never failed to cheer us up. We pray and trust that he has been liberated into the heart of Amitabha.

GLOSSARY

ajahn (Th.; P. *acarya*)   Teacher.

Ajahn Mun (1870–1950)   The most renowned meditation master of the previous century in Thailand, and the teacher of most of the great masters in northeast Thailand in Ajahn Chah's generation.

almsround (P. *pindapata*)   The Theravadin monastic custom of leaving the monastery every morning to seek almsfood. Monks stand in silence with their almsbowls outside of a house long enough to determine if the residents will offer anything. In Thailand, donors are usually lined up outside, waiting for the monks.

anatta (P.)   The lack of a true, permanent self inherent in, constituted by, or owning the factors of body and mind.

anicca (P.)   Impermanence; often translated by Ajahn Chah as "uncertainty."

arahant (P.)   The final level of enlightenment in Theravada Buddhism. Literally, "the one far from the afflictions" or "the one who has destroyed the enemy."

(P.: Pali; Skt.: Sanskrit; Th.: Thai)

ariyas (P.)   The Noble Ones, those who have attained the levels of enlightenment and thus are no longer ordinary beings.

bhikkhu (P.)   A fully ordained monk. Literally, "one who sees danger in the round of samsara."

bodhi tree   The tree (*ficus religiosa*) beneath which the Buddha sat when he attained enlightenment, in Bodh Gaya, India. *Bodhi* (P.) means "enlightenment."

bodhisattva (Skt.; P. *bodhisatta*)   An "awakening being," one who has taken the vow to become a buddha for the sake of liberating others. In Theravada teachings, "The Bodhisatta" refers specifically to the past lives of the Buddha when he was developing the spiritual perfections to become a buddha.

Buddho (P.)   The name of the Buddha, commonly used as a meditation object in Thailand, meaning "the one who knows."

deathless, the   The state beyond suffering, beyond the round of birth and death; nirvana.

defilements (P. *kilesa*)   The mental afflictions of desire, aversion, and delusion.

Dharma (Skt.; P. *Dhamma*)   (With uppercase *D*.)The teaching of the Buddha; the truth; ultimate truth.

dharma   (With lowercase *d*.) Phenomena. Literally, "that which exists."

dukkha (P.)   Unsatisfactoriness, the suffering nature of existence; the first of the Four Noble Truths taught by the Buddha.

eighth rebirth   The last rebirth. One who enters the stream to nirvana will be reborn no more than seven times before attaining final enlightenment.

four foundations of mindfulness   The basic meditation system in Theravada Buddhism, which includes mindfulness of the body, feelings, mind, and dharmas.

Four Noble Truths   The first teaching of the Buddha: the truths of suffering, its origin, its cessation, and the path leading out of suffering.

jhana (P.)   Meditative absorption, states of deep concentration usually classified into eight stages, the four jhanas of form and the four formless jhanas.

khandha (P.)   Aggregate: the classification of psychophysical components—bodily form, feelings, memory/perception, volitional thinking, and consciousness—mistakenly thought to constitute a person or self. Literally, "heap."

kuti (P.)   Monastic dwelling, usually a small cabin raised on pillars.

lower realms   States of extreme suffering. Usually referring to animals, hungry spirits, and hell, it can also mean the extreme mental suffering of humans.

Luang Por (Th.)   Title of respect and affection for an older monk. Literally, "Revered Father."

merit (P. *punya*)   Positive qualities of mind and the activities that accumulate them.

metta (P.)   Loving-kindness; impartially wishing happiness for all, including oneself.

nirvana (Skt.; P. *nibbana*)   The enlightened state, the unconditioned; the extinction of desire, aversion, and delusion.

pacceka buddha (P.)   One who attains enlightenment without a teacher and does not have the ability to teach others; usually depicted as living in solitude.

Pali   The dialect of Sanskrit in which the Buddha taught.

perfections (P. *paramis*)   Spiritual qualities that are cultivated as a support for realizing enlightenment. In Theravada Buddhism, there are ten: generosity, morality, renunciation, wisdom, effort, forbearance, truthfulness, resolution, loving kindness, and equanimity.

samadhi (P.)   Concentration; meditative stability.

samatha (P.)   Tranquillity meditation.

samsara (Skt.; P. *sangsara*)   The round of birth and death, the cycle of unsatisfactory conditioned existence.

Sangha (P.)   The community of those who practice the Buddha's way. It can refer to any group of Buddhists, whether lay or monastic. The Sangha as an object of refuge (along with the Buddha and the Dharma) refers to those who have realized enlightenment.

sankhara (P.)   All conditioned phenomena, that is, anything that has a beginning and an end, birth and death. As the fourth of the aggregates, it refers to thought or mental formations. In the Thai vernacular, it can refer to the body.

self-conceit (P. *mana*)   The basic sense of self; feeling that one is anything at all is a mental fetter that is only removed with realization of the arahant stage.

sila (P.)   Virtue or morality, and the code of conduct and precepts that is in accord with and leads to virtue.

stream enterer (P. *sotapanna*)   One who attains the first level of enlightenment. Having entered the stream to full enlightenment, this person will be reborn seven times at most.

Tathagata (P.)   An epithet for the Buddha. Literally, "the One Thus Gone."

tudong (Th.; P. *dhutanga*)   Ascetic observances permitted for Theravadin monks. It commonly refers to the practice of leaving the monastery and wandering in forests and charnel grounds and traveling on foot to visit meditation teachers and monasteries.

Ubon   The province in northeast Thailand where Ajahn Chah lived and where Ajahn Mun was born. Also the name of the provincial capital, about five miles from Wat Pah Pong, Ajahn Chah's monastery.

vipassana (P.)   Insight meditation. Literally, "special seeing."

Visakha Puja (P.)   Holiday commemorating the Buddha's birth, enlightenment, and death (*parinirvana*).

wat (Th.)   Monastery.

Wat Pah Pong   Ajahn Chah's main monastery, founded in 1954 in a dense forest about one and a half miles from his home village.

zazen   Zen sitting meditation.

RESOURCES

Readers interested in learning more about the Thai Forest Tradition may go to *www.forestsangha.org* or contact the monasteries listed below for information on Ajahn Chah, his monasteries and teachings, and the teachings and activities of his disciples.

Australia
   Bodhinyana Monastery
   216 Kingsbury Drive
   Serpentine WA 6125, Australia
   (61)(0)8 9525 2420

Italy
   Santacittarama Monastero Buddhista
   Località Brulla
   02030 Frasso Sabino (RI), Italy
   (39)(0)765 872 186

New Zealand
   Bodhinyanarama Forest Monastery
   17 Rakau Grove
   Stokes Valley
   Wellington, New Zealand
   (64)(0)4 563 7193

Switzerland

Dhammapala Buddhistisches Kloster
Am Waldrand
378 Kandersteg, CH-3718, Switzerland
(41)(033)675 2100

Thailand

Wat Pah Nanachat (International Forest Monastery)
Bahn Bung Wai
Amper Warin
Ubon Province 34310, Thailand

UK

Amaravati Buddhist Monastery
St. Margaret's Lane
Great Gaddesden
Hemel Hempstead
Hertfordshire HP1 3BZ, UK

Aruna Ratanagiri Buddhist Monastery
2 Harnham Hall Cottages
Harnham, Belsay
Northumberland NE 20 0HF, UK

Cittaviveka
Chithurst Buddhist Monastery
Chithurst (W. Sussex), Petersfield
Hampshire GU 31 5EU, UK
(44) 01404 89 1251

Devon Vihara
Hartridge Buddhist Monastery
Odle Cottage
Upottery, Honiton
Devon EX 14 9QE, UK

USA

Abhayagiri Buddhist Monastery
16201 Tomki Road
Redwood Valley, CA 95470, USA
(1)(707)485-1630

ABOUT THE TRANSLATOR

BORN IN BROOKLYN IN 1948, Paul Breiter traveled to Thailand in 1970, where he took ordination as a monk. Shortly thereafter, he met Ajahn Chah and became his student. Breiter learned Thai and the local Lao dialect (Isan) and served as Ajahn Chah's translator for the many Westerners who came to study with him. He kept a journal of his translations of Ajahn Chah's teachings, some of which he published with Jack Kornfield in *A Still Forest Pool* (Quest Books, 1985). He also translated a volume of the *Vinayamukha,* a text on monastic discipline (*Entrance to the Vinaya,* Vol. III; Mahamakuta Royal Academy, 1983). Breiter traveled with and translated for Ajahn Chah when he visited the United States in 1979. He later published an account of his time studying with Ajahn Chah called *Venerable Father: A Life with Ajahn Chah* that has become an underground classic (self-published, 1993; Buddhadhamma Foundation, 1994; Paraview Press, 2004).

After disrobing in 1977, Breiter returned to the United States and continued his Buddhist studies with Roshi Kobun Chino Otogawa of the Soto Zen school, and then with Lama Gonpo Tsedan of the Nyingmapa lineage of Tibetan Buddhism. He currently lives in Florida.